© Paleo Canteen 2020
Cover Art by Rekha Barry
Photography by Clair Irwin

Praise For
Low Carb On A Budget

'I thought I didn't need another cookbook, but this is a must-have. The authors are such persuasive ambassadors for this sane, healthy, and affordable way of eating that makes my mouth water. Such a lucid and helpful explanation of the virtues of a paleo approach to food, with lipsmacking recipes that won't break the bank'.
- Joanna Blythman, Restaurant critic, investigative journalist, and 2018 Food Writer of the Year

'As a doctor, I'm always looking for ways to help my patients out. When I wrote my best selling book The Pioppi Diet, I explained how we can eat healthily by cooking for ourselves. This book has some of the finest recipes I've ever seen, and all within a budget that will allow anyone to enjoy. I won't just be recommending this book to my patients, I'll be recommending it to all my family and friends, and using it myself. Essential reading!'.
- Dr. Aseem Malhotra, Cardiologist and best-selling author of 'The Pioppi Diet'

'The Paleo Canteen Team have produced a beautifully illustrated essential cookbook. Tasty cuisine from top chefs who understand the need to keep the Paleo way of eating affordable. Eat well, enjoy cooking, lose weight and save money. Highly recommended'.
- Dr. Andrew Jenkinson, Bariatric Surgeon and author of the Sunday Times Bestseller 'Why We Eat (Too Much) - The New Science of Appetite'

''Paleo Canteen - Low Carb on a Budget' is a fantastic resource for anyone wanting to take back control of their health. John and Ally's amazing recipes are based on affordable, nutrient dense ingredients proving that Paleo and Low Carb lifestyles don't need to be expensive or restrictive. Invest in your health today!'.

- Belinda Fettke, international speaker on food and nutrition

'You guys have done a great job. The recipes are mouth watering'.
- Dr. Peter Brukner, author and former doctor to the Australian cricket team and Liverpool FC

'I think your cookbook is charming! I love the focus on budget-friendly meals - and I especially love the fact that you don't take "budget-friendly" to mean "boring." Altogether, it is a collection of recipes that will have both the readers and the eaters asking for "More, please!"'.

- Dr. Adele Hite, MPH, RDN, registered dietitian with a masters' degree in public health nutrition

'This book has delicious and truly original recipes that will suit low carbers and those following a paleo diet. There are no school dinner reproductions here. Both authors are trained and experienced chefs and their use of accompanying vegetables, herbs and spices lift the meals into restaurant quality fare. Low carb eating can transform your health, particularly if you have diabetes, and this book provides a useful part in making the experience a highly enjoyable one, whether you have health problems or not'.

- Dr Katharine Morrison, founder member of PHC, author of 'The Diabetes Diet'

To Sarit, Trish and Rory - thanks for teaching me to cook.

- **John**

To Rekha - thanks for everything.

- **Ally**

Contents

FOREWORD
Dr. David Unwin

I am a family doctor working in a seaside town north of Liverpool since 1986. From then until 2012 I was aware of a rising tide of obesity and hypertension with an eight-fold increase in type 2 diabetes. All the drugs I prescribed seemed to be merely 'sticking plasters' rather than a true solution to these problems, so I became disillusioned with general practice and prepared to retire.

Then one patient walked in and changed my life. She had put her diabetes into drug-free remission simply by cutting not just sugar but the starchy carbs that digest down into sugar. Fascinated, I went on the diet myself and found my blood pressure and middle aged spread both improved in weeks.

Since 2012 millions of people round the world have 'cut the carbs' including hundreds of my own patients. A few weeks ago I saw the 73rd practice patient to achieve significant weight loss and drug-free type 2 diabetes remission. As a bonus the diet has cured her swollen ankles too!

I'm often asked if this is an expensive, middle class diet. Firstly to be fair you should factor in what you currently spend on cans of drink, snacks, biscuits and other 'food-like substances' - you will be saving in this department. Secondly on the whole green veg is not expensive. To go low carb cheaply it is important to look at less expensive forms of protein like chicken, mince and other cheaper cuts of meat, eggs or cheese. For this you have to be a little more creative – hence this little book to get you started.

N.B. for those on regular medication for diabetes or blood pressure: because low carb diets tend to drop blood sugars and improve blood pressure, it's important to discuss your new diet with a health care professional. Medication may need changing or, even if you are lucky, stopping altogether.

Cheers,

David.

PROUD TO SUPPORT THE

The Public Health Collaboration is a registered charity dedicated to informing and implementing healthy decisions for better public health. They publish evidence-based reports on the most pressing public health issues alongside coordinated campaigns and implementing initiatives for improving public health.

The director of the PHC is Samuel Feltham. In March 2016, Sam closed his fitness boot camp business to fully focus on running the Public Health Collaboration. In the past few years of being in the health and fitness industry he noticed an increasing number of doctors coming out of the woodwork to support real food and smart exercise to treat and prevent diseases and conditions, instead of just prescribing drugs and pushing fake food.

He started having conversations with many of the Public Health Collaboration founding members about how they can start creating real change in the UK for improving the health of the nation, which is getting worse year upon year despite all of our best efforts. The one thing that they kept going back to was to collaborate their efforts into one singular organisation to inform the public and empower the medical community on the science and solutions of health.

Over a melting pot of ideas they founded the Public Health Collaboration, or the PHC for short.

We are delighted to be supporting the PHC on Paleo Canteen Low Carb On A Budget. For every full length cookbook we sell Paleo Canteen will donate 50p to the PHC so that they can continue their incredible work.

INTRODUCTION
John Meechan

I've been a chef for a fair amount of time now, but it wasn't until I met Ally about two years ago that I began to consider the nutritional aspect of food. This wasn't so much out of necessity – I'm in good health, and don't react noticeably badly to anything other than caffeine – as out of curiosity, and the desire for a new challenge. I'd just finished a PhD in philosophy, and suddenly found myself with a lot of spare mind-energy; alongside this, I was at a bit of a crossroads in terms of my cooking career, keen to start doing something of my own after years of working under others. The low carb diet intrigued me intellectually, and appeared to offer a route into the world of human nutrition in a way that made a lot of sense to me. At the same time, the limitations and stipulations it offered in the kitchen motivated me creatively – it raised seasonal, nose-to-tail cooking to an imperative. I decided to give it a try.

It took some getting used to. I don't have much of a sweet tooth, but there are few savoury foods I don't like, so letting go of things like polenta, rice, and chickpeas was a big deal to begin with. But soon enough I realised that a low carb diet actually implores you to eat some of my favourite ingredients, and at that point I was sold.

Cue slow-roast pork belly aplenty, piles of spring greens doused in olive oil, smoked mackerel and

9

buttery eggs in the morning, beef mince in as many ways as you can imagine. The benefits soon followed. I felt unexpectedly stabilised both mentally and physically, able to focus better, less prone to ups and downs. I also felt my hunger come under control, which was an added bonus, and contributed significantly to the newfound sense of resilience I was experiencing. It now seems a no-brainer to me that the right diet will let you go several hours in between meals without energy crashes or cravings for quick fixes.

Changing to a low carb diet involves changing the way you cook, both in terms of the way you shop and the way you respond to your appetite. Our particular aim with this set of recipes is to show you that this change need neither put burdensome constraints on how you eat, nor squeeze your budget when shopping. We know this first-hand because we live on tight budgets as well as low carb diets, but refuse to let either of these things get in the way of eating well. Dieting may be a necessity, depending on your circumstances, but the joys of cooking and eating don't have to suffer. Indeed, once you've made your peace with the ingredients you've been advised to eliminate and embraced a broadly wholefoods principle, you'll find that

the range of what remains open to you is both fair on your pocket and conducive to delicious meals.

It may help, to begin with, to adopt a fairly formulaic approach: choose a meat or fish, pair it with a seasonal vegetable or two, and bring these together with a garnish that will add colour, freshness and flavour. Within this, of course, the possibilities are vast, whether in terms of the combinations you opt for or the length of time you wish to invest in preparing a dish. But I hope you'll find that, with this basic formula in mind, alongside a larder cupboard stocked with a few basic essentials, you can create tasty meals that benefit your health, work within your budget, and don't over-complicate your life in the kitchen.

John Meechan trained as a chef in London, notably under Yotam Ottolenghi, Sarit Packer & Itamar Srulovich and Trish Hilferty. He lives in Glasgow, where he runs a broadly low carb pop-up restaurant called The Mustard Spoon.

Ally Houston

My first job when I left school was in Rogano, a fine dining seafood restaurant in Glasgow, the oldest surviving restaurant in the city. The managers took a boy who was fed well at home but, left to his own devices, ate nothing but beige processed food, and taught him what it means to appreciate the best that food can offer. I worked in high end restaurants for several years, working my way up to managerial positions. I then went to university and got a physics degree.

The professors took a young man who thought he knew everything and taught him the principles of scientific inquiry.

My health had always been up and down. My Mum says that we had a season ticket to the children's hospital. Several of my family members and I have had serious autoimmune diseases, mine requiring surgery twice. Heart disease and Alzheimer's runs in my family.

Things had gotten really bad in 2015 during my studying for a PhD in physics. I couldn't focus, and found myself to be frequently

anxious and depressed. One of my supervisors, Professor Ken Strain, had healed his chronic fatigue syndrome / ME using a change in diet, and shared information, showing me how to access scientific papers on nutrition online.

Like so many before and since, I was astonished by what I was reading. If you have a scientific background and a curiosity about food, it's difficult to come to any other conclusions than the following three.

- Sugar, refined flour, and vegetable (seed) oils are extremely harmful to human health.
- Eating foods that provide the required nutrients is as healthy a diet as you can get.
- Switching to a low carbohydrate diet can bring huge benefits for certain people, especially if the person has type two diabetes or chronic metabolic health problems.

When I changed how I ate to a paleo low carbohydrate diet, my health improved dramatically. I left my PhD in physics to pursue my first love, food.

Fast forward more than two years, and Paleo Canteen has become a name that our customers can trust. We focus on providing the highest quality food that encourages good health.

Sometimes it can be hard to eat healthily and stay within your budget. That's why myself and John wanted to write this book. We have combined our collective experience in some of the UK's best restaurants, and our experience of the benefits of a low carb lifestyle, into a collection of recipes that allow you to maximise your health without breaking the bank.

How did we decide what qualifies as budget low carb food? We chose lamb mince as an upper limit for meat price. If it costs less than lamb mince, it made it into the book. But even that can seem expensive, so how can we justify the title of the book?

As you read in the foreword, Dr. Unwin's patients have achieved an unprecedented rate of drug free Type 2 diabetes remission. This rate is similar to those in the Virta Health study in the U.S. which also uses a low carb diet to improve Type 2 diabetes and achieve drug free remission. There is a growing number of success stories online in the various social media groups dedicated to low carb. We see how powerful this way of eating is. We believe that this power justifies a different perspective on "value for money" when it comes to buying food.

The way I think about it is in terms of nutrition per £, per €, or per $. Yes, you can buy a box of pasta for 50p or 60c, and get hundreds of calories of energy, but how much nutrition is in there? Very little! In fact, it's worse than that. Because flour prevents nutrient absorption in the gut, and because nutrients can be stripped out during processing, nutrients have to be added to avoid deficiencies.

So, it might cost 50p/60c for a pasta meal, and £3/$4 for a lamb mince meal, but in terms of nutrition, the lamb wins hands down, and you won't be storing up problems for the future or stoking the fires of inflammation that already exist in you. There are other ways to get the best value. Look out for times of the day when shops reduce the price on food. You can pick up some real bargains on meat at these times.

There are ways to get enough nutrients and protein without eating meat, fish, and eggs, but supplementation becomes important at that point, and we wanted to focus on getting all of our nutrition from food. This is why we don't focus on vegetarian or vegan options.

Dairy was another important consideration. Paleo people are dairy free, and those who do have dairy but otherwise stick to paleo principles would call themselves primal. John and I love adding some dairy to our diets. I tend to only have some double cream or the occasional mouthful of yoghurt or creme fraiche. Others enjoy cheese without any negative effects. If that applies to you, go for it!

Ally Houston is the founder and director of Paleo Canteen, the UK's premium paleo and low carb food company.

A NOTE ON THE RECIPES

If there's one thing I'd like to encourage in the recipes that follow, it's an intuitive relationship to your ingredients and how you select and prepare them for your meals. I've always valued this as a chef, as it helps maintain creativity and seasonality, but on the home front I found that it came increasingly to the fore when I began eating low carb. This is probably because cooking this way requires you to work with a determined range of ingredients.

When shopping, I'd typically buy the things that I knew were good for me, then think about what to make with them when I got home. Of course, this doesn't have to be your approach – perhaps you prefer to plan meals in advance of shopping for them – but you may well find that a degree of flexibility develops by itself once you get used to the main staples.

To that end, we've tried to approach this book as something like an instruction manual, in the sense that it provides the basis for a host of meals, using a repertoire of ingredients that comply with the low carb diet and are generally plentiful and affordable, and emphasises a margin of variability for you to alter things in line with your own preferences.

In many of the recipes, I leave open the question of quantities, and sometimes of specific ingredients like herbs, because I think it's important to determine these yourself on the basis of how hungry you are, what flavours or ingredients you like accentuated, and also what you have in your fridge, freezer and cupboards.

Resourcefulness is an indispensable quality in the kitchen, and not only when you're cooking on a budget: it's a fertile source of creativity, and often the bridge between what you want to eat and what you're able to cook.

SHOPPING LOW CARB: STAPLES & STORE CUPBOARDS

The difference between cooking interesting and average food can sometimes come down to what you have in your larder. This becomes especially pertinent when eating on a budget: a little initial investment will allow you to turn a single fresh ingredient or two into something unexpectedly satisfying. Below is a list of items it's worth stocking up on, not only for the recipes that follow – you'll find these ingredients crop up again and again – but also far beyond. Think of them as a toolbox for adding flavour and depth to your cooking.

Non-perishables

Capers
Anchovies
Tinned tuna
Mustards: Dijon and wholegrain
Tomato puree
Tahini
Vinegars: white or red wine, sherry, distilled malt
Coconut milk (high fat)
Tinned chopped tomatoes
Honey or Puresweet

Dark chocolate (at least 70% cocoa solids)

Perishables

Garlic
Red chillies
Lemons
Parmesan cheese
High-fat Yogurt, Greek style or natural

Spices

It's worth saying that you'll get a noticeably better flavour from your spices by buying them in seed form, toasting them lightly, then grinding them just prior to use. However, there's not always the time or will to do this, and using pre-ground powders is perfectly fine.
Cumin
Oregano
Cinnamon
Paprika, regular and smoked
Coriander
Caraway
Cloves

Nutmeg
Turmeric
Allspice
White pepper
Star anise
Mustard seeds, brown and yellow

Seeds

Pumpkin
Linseed
Chia
Sesame
Sunflower
Poppy

Nuts

Buying nuts in meal or flaked form is great if you're planning on baking, but it's often cheaper and more versatile to buy them whole and then ground or chop them as you require.
Hazelnuts
Almonds
Brazil nuts
Desiccated coconut

Fats

Since we have to get our energy from somewhere, it stands to reason that cutting down carbs means increasing our fat intake. Consuming fatty meat and fish is the best way to ensure this, but it also impacts on the kinds of oils and fats we use to cook with.

Just as a calorie is never just a calorie – compare the qualitative difference between a calorie of pizza and a calorie of lamb mince – it's important to select the right kinds of fats in the kitchen. Veg oils, most nuts, and animals fed lots of grains (like chicken and pork) contain an omega 6 fat called linoleic acid (LA). Although this is present in all wholefoods, it is found in much higher levels in the foods just mentioned.

In our evolution, we didn't have access to veg oils at all, it's unlikely we would have had easy and year-round access to lots of nuts, and animals like pigs would have been eating a wide variety of foods besides grains. When we look at the level of LA in the diets of modern hunter-gatherers we find that it's uniformly low, whereas when we look at the level of LA in westernised cultures, it's much higher. There's lots of good evidence to suggest that consuming levels of LA above a few percent of daily calories can be extremely damaging to health. There's also good evidence that LA is less harmful when on a low carb diet, as sugar will bring out more of the toxic by-products of LA.

Day-to-day, what does this mean for you? Well, broadly speaking, if you focus your low carb diet on red meat, fish and eggs, and enjoy chicken, pork and nuts a few times a week alongside these, while avoiding veg oils altogether, you'll be doing yourself a big favour. More specifically for your cooking, however, it means you should try to limit yourself to the following:

Beef dripping

Beef dripping is great: it not only has a high smoke point, but can be used repeatedly without degrading, and most importantly has very little of the worst omega 6 fat found in veg oils. It also tastes wonderful when cooked into your favourite dishes.

Coconut oil

Coconut is not high in LA, and therefore makes a completely safe cooking oil. It can have a mild coconut flavour, so is well suited to curries and other tropical dishes. You'll see expensive options for extra virgin coconut oil, but there's no need to shell out on this – the standard versions are perfectly good.

Olive oil

Extra virgin olive oil (EVOO) is made from the fruit rather than the seed, so unlike other oils made from vegetables, it is much lower in LA. You can cook with olive oil safely, but where possible it's best to substitute with dripping or coconut oil. Heating increases the most harmful form of LA and so olive oil is well suited to cold dishes, and of course tastes delicious. You'll also find 'light' olive oil in most shops. This is typically made from the 'pomace', which contains the skins, pulp, seeds and stems of the fruit, and as such has higher levels of LA than EVOO. We use this sometimes for things like mayonnaise, but you don't have to – EVOO is perfectly fine if you like the stronger flavour.

Butter

Butter is a supremely delicious and versatile fat – it can be whipped, browned, emulsified, foamed or just spread - and it brings irresistible flavour to almost anything you add it to. For these reasons, like much other dairy, it can easily be overeaten. Used as one of many options within your low carb diet, however, it's a valuable source of saturated fat. If you can, try to buy butter made from pasture-raised cows, which will raise its nutritional value.

Lastly, be sure to save any excess fat that renders off meat that you're frying or roasting. You can store this in the fridge and use it as the basis of later meals.

Stocks

There's nothing wrong with using dried stock cubes, but making your own will add an extra layer of flavour to your cooking and an extra string to your bow in the kitchen.

You'll find many detailed and precise recipes for stocks in books and online, and there certainly is an art to making them to a high standard, but it's also worth bearing in mind, especially when you're cooking on a budget, that they are at bottom water flavoured with bones (and usually some vegetables and herbs), and that even the simplest improvised broth will enhance a braise tenfold or give you a basic sauce with little effort.

So it's worth getting into the habit of keeping any bones that are left when preparing a meal, asking your butcher or fishmonger if they have any bones that day, and keeping any vegetable trim to add to the pot.

Beef, chicken, lamb or pork stock

Roast the bones in a hot oven until they're nice and golden.
Meantime, depending on what you have in the fridge, chop up any combination of onion, carrot, celery, leek and or/garlic. In a pot that's big enough to hold everything, fry off the vegetables in some beef dripping, olive oil, or –ideally – any fat that renders off the roasting bones. You just want the vegetables to soften and get some colour.

Once the bones are coloured, add them to the pot, along with any fat that's gathered in the roasting dish, and cover with water.

Again depending on what you have, add some bay, rosemary, thyme, and/or black peppercorns, but never salt.

Bring the stock up to a gentle simmer, removing any scum that rises to the surface with a ladle. It's fine to leave the fat there as it contributes flavour, just be careful not to boil the water or the fat may emulsify into it.

From here you can judge its readiness by the smell and flavour, and be sure to top up the water if it ever gets too low during the cooking process. A stock made with the carcass of a roast chicken will be ready to use within an hour (though will benefit from a longer braise), whereas one made with beef marrow bones will take much longer (wait for the bones to go hollow).

Once it's ready, strain through as fine a sieve as you have. You can store it as it is, or reduce it down if you want to intensify the flavour or make it easier to store.

Fish stock

The best bones for fish stock are from white, mild-flavoured fish like cod, sole, haddock, halibut, hake or pollock. It's best to just tell your fishmonger that's what you want to make and they should be able to provide you with something suitable. Place them in a pot and add enough water to just cover them. Depending on what you have available, add any combination of white onion, celery, fennel and/or leek, alongside bay, parsley and/or black peppercorns.

Bring up to just below the boil, skim off any froth that rises to the surface, then turn down to a very gentle simmer for half an hour. Remove from the heat and leave to rest for another half hour before carefully straining through as fine a sieve as you have.

MINCE: SOME CLASSICS REVISITED

Lamb koftas with roast cauliflower salad
Beef chilli with kale
Shepherd's pie
Spaghetti meatballs with courgetti
Pork patties in broth
Lamb faggots with minted peas

Mince (or ground meat) is the cheap, fatty meat par excellence, and something of a go-to for us. It's versatile, comforting, and will make you a satisfying meal in five minutes if you're short on time. These recipes provide low carb renditions of some familiar dishes using beef, lamb and pork mince.

Lamb koftas with roast cauliflower salad

These little spiced meatballs really satisfy a craving for charred, fatty, flavourful meat. If you're able to do them on the barbeque they'll be even better. The herby cauliflower salad on the side is a great foil for the koftas – punchy, sweet, and with a little crunch from the almonds.

Feeds 2-3

500g / 18oz high-fat lamb mince / ground lamb (beef works too)
1 onion
2 cloves of garlic, minced
1.5 tsp salt
1 small cauliflower
½ a pomegranate
60g / 1/3 cup flaked almonds
A handful of fresh coriander, chopped
A handful of fresh dill, chopped
A lemon
Extra virgin olive oil
Yogurt

Spice mix:
1 tsp ground cumin
1.5 tsp ground cinnamon
1.5 tsp ground allspice
1 tsp black pepper
1/2 tsp grated nutmeg

Pre-heat the oven to 220C / Fan 200 / Gas 7 / 425F, and have an oven tray lined with parchment ready.

To make the koftas, grate the onion and squeeze out as much liquid as you can through a sieve. Combine this with the mince, garlic, and all but a teaspoon of the spice mix in a bowl and knead until everything is well mixed together and pliable. Shape them into 10 oblong shapes, and refrigerate while you prepare the cauliflower.

Break the cauliflower into florets, being sure to tear off some stalk with each piece. Ideally they'll be similar in size so that they cook evenly. Place in a bowl with the remaining 1 tsp of spice mix. Season with salt, drizzle with olive oil, spread over your baking tray, and roast for around 15 minutes, or until it's taken on a golden colour and you can pierce through the stalk with a sharp knife. Remove from the oven, which you can now turn down to 150 C.

Put a griddle pan onto a high heat. If you don't have one, a heavy-based frying pan is fine.

Once the oven has come down to temperature, toast the flaked almonds until golden (up to 10 minutes, tossing halfway through).

Put the cauliflower in a bowl, pouring in any olive oil from the roasting dish. Add the zest and juice of half the lemon, along with the seeds of the pomegranate and the toasted almonds. Toss everything around, and leave the flavours to merge.

Take your koftas from the fridge and start cooking them in the griddle pan. You may have to do this in a couple of batches. (If using a frying pan, add a little oil first.) Allow them to colour on one side before turning them and doing the same with the other side. When you're satisfied with the colour, remove them to an oven tray, and give them 5 minutes in the oven to finish off. If you're unsure as to whether they're cooked, simply slice into one to check.

Depending on how you shaped them, you may indeed find that they don't require any further cooking in the oven.

To serve, toss the fresh herbs through the cauliflower salad and check for seasoning – it may need an extra squeeze of lemon juice, more salt, or a glug of olive oil. Share among the plates along with the koftas, and top with a dollop of yogurt.

Net carbs for whole recipe is 30.9g. For each serving, simply divide this weight by number of servings.

Beef chilli with kale

This is a rich, deep-tasting chilli that will make you wonder why you ever needed rice alongside it. If you have some left, warm it up with fried eggs in the morning.

Serves 2-3

500g / 18oz high-fat beef mince / ground beef
70g / 2.5oz chorizo, diced
1 onion, finely diced
3 cloves of garlic, minced
1 red chilli, sliced
1 tsp dried oregano
1 tsp ground cumin
½ tsp ground cinnamon
½ tsp smoked paprika
½ tsp dried chilli flakes
1tbsp tomato puree
1 tin chopped tomatoes (400g / 2 cups)
25g / 1/8 cup dark chocolate (around 80% cocoa), chopped
Red or white wine vinegar

To garnish:
4 big handfuls of kale leaves
Yogurt or sour cream
Spring onions
Fresh coriander

If using an oven-proof pot, preheat the oven to 150 C / Fan 130 / Gas 2 / 300 F.

Place a pot on a high heat, and once it's up to temperature start browning the mince all over. Once it's taken on some colour and any released water has evaporated, add the chorizo, onions, garlic, chilli and spices, season everything well with salt, and allow leave to cook out, stirring occasionally, until you can see that the onion has softened.

Add the tomato puree, stir through, and allow to cook out for 2 minutes before adding the chopped tomatoes. Fill the tin up halfway with water in order to rinse out the remaining tomato juice and add this to the pot too. Allow everything to come up to the boil, check the seasoning, then put the lid on and either cook in the oven for 45 minutes, or on a low heat for the same time, being sure to stir it occasionally throughout.

When the time's up, remove from the oven, take off the lid, give it a stir around, and leave it to settle while you cook the kale.

Put a pot of water on to boil. Chop

the kale up roughly, salt the water once it's up to temperature, then cook the kale for 3-4 minutes, depending on how tough the leaves are. If you're unsure, eat a piece to test it. Once you're happy, strain it off and allow to drip-dry for a couple of minutes.

Go back to your chilli and stir through the chocolate until melted, then check a final time for seasoning: it may need a little more salt, and a splash of vinegar will do it good.

To serve, place some kale in a bowl and spoon over the chilli. Garnish with a dollop of yogurt and some chopped spring onions and coriander.

Net carbs for whole recipe is 40.6g. For each serving, simply divide this weight by number of servings.

Shepherd's pie

Here the traditional mashed potato topping is replaced with celeriac – not as creamy but just as satisfying.

Serves 2-3

500g / 18oz high-fat lamb mince / ground lamb
1 onion
1 large carrot
2 sprigs of rosemary
500ml / 2 cups chicken or lamb stock
1 large celeriac
50g / 1/4 cup butter
1 tbsp wholegrain mustard
1 egg

Put a pot of water on to boil for the celeriac.
On a high heat, brown the lamb mince in a little olive oil or beef dripping, seasoned with salt and pepper.

In the meantime, dice the onion and carrot. Once the lamb's lost its moisture and taken on some colour, remove it from the pan and start sweating down the vegetables, seasoned, on a low-medium heat with a lid on. Give it 5-10 minutes, just until soft, then return the lamb mince along with the rosemary, stripped from the stalk and chopped.

Add the stock, bring to the boil and check for seasoning. Put the lid on but leave it slightly ajar, and cook on a low heat for 45 minutes.

During this time, peel the celeriac, cut into even-sized chunks and wash in case there's still some dirt attached to it. Salt the boiling water (a heaped teaspoon) and cook the celeriac until you're able to pierce the chunks easily with a knife. Strain, return to the pot, and mash along with the butter, mustard, and any extra seasoning you think it needs. Whisk the egg in a separate bowl then whisk it through the mash. Set aside while the lamb finishes cooking.

Pre-heat the oven to 180C / Fan 160 / Gas 4 / 350F.

Once the 45 minutes are up, remove the lid from the lamb and check the liquid levels. If there's still a lot, raise the heat and let more of it bubble away – you want there to be sauce, but not for the mince to be swimming.

Transfer the mince to an appropriately sized oven dish, then top with the celeriac mash.

Sit the dish on a tray (to catch any liquid that jumps out) and place in the oven for around 20 minutes, or until the top is nicely coloured and the juice underneath is starting to bubble through.

Net carbs for whole recipe is 54g. For each serving, simply divide this weight by number of servings.

Spaghetti meatballs with courgetti

For various reasons, we've never been fans of contriving substitutes for things you're no longer supposed to eat – cauliflower 'pizza base', cashew 'cheese' – but spaghetti-like strips of courgette are an exception: it's a tasty way to eat them and they remain after all a wholefood. Just be sure to let some liquid drip off before you serve them up.

Serves 2-3

500g / 18oz high-fat beef mince / ground beef
1 small onion, grated
4 cloves of garlic, minced
2 tsp dried oregano
1 egg, lightly beaten
1½tsp salt
1 tin chopped tomatoes (400g / 2 cups)
1 bay leaf
2 courgettes / zucchinis, peeled with a julienne peeler, or spiralised
A small handful of fresh basil
Parmesan (optional)

Set the oven to 200C / Fan 180 / Gas 6 / 400F.
For the meatballs, combine the mince, onion, half the garlic, oregano, egg and salt in a bowl and knead until everything is well mixed together and pliable into balls.

Shape the mix into 12 meatballs and place them on an oven tray large enough to allow 2 fingers space in between them. Roast them in the oven for around 20 minutes, or until they've taken on some colour.

Meantime prepare the sauce. On a low heat, warm the remaining garlic in some olive oil in a pot that will be large enough to hold the meatballs. It only needs to get going a little, and shouldn't be allowed to colour – 10-20 seconds. Now add the tomatoes and bay leaf and bring up to a simmer. Season with salt and pepper, then allow the sauce to cook until the meatballs are out the oven.

Once they're nicely coloured, add the meatballs to the sauce, arrange neatly, cover with a lid or tinfoil, and cook on a very low heat for 45 minutes. You can do this in the oven if your pot is oven-proof – just turn it down to 150.
While this is cooking, peel your courgettes with the julienne peeler,

which will turn them into long, spaghetti-like strands. Or, spiralise them with a spiraliser. They'll lose their volume a little when you fry them off, so don't worry if you appear to have too much.

Once the meatballs have cooked, remove from the heat and set aside. The sauce may be a little thick. Add 100-200ml of hot water to loosen the sauce out if need be.

Put a wide-based frying pan or pot on a high heat and, once it's hot, add a little olive oil and flash-fry the courgette, seasoning with salt. The aim here is simply to take the rawness off them rather than to thoroughly cook them, as they'll wilt down too much if you do this. Continue shifting them around the pan as they cook, and they'll be done in less than a minute. Remove from the heat and sit in a colander over a sink for a minute.

To serve, chop the basil through the courgettes and distribute among bowls. Top with the meatballs and a good ladleful of sauce. Shave over some parmesan if you have it.

Net carbs for whole recipe is 29.4g. For each serving, simply divide this weight by number of servings.

Pork patties in broth

This is great comfort food – quick to prepare and delicious. If the lettuce isn't enough for you, try replacing it with chard, which is a little more robust.

Serves 2-3

500g / 180oz pork mince / ground pork
1 egg
1 large shallot
3 anchovies
2 cloves of garlic
1 tsp fennel seeds, freshly ground
½ tsp black peppercorns, freshly ground
A handful of fresh herbs, such as parsley, chives or basil
A lemon
Around 500ml / 2 cups of chicken stock
2 heads of round lettuce

Warm the chicken stock up in a pot while you make the patties.
Mince the shallot, garlic and anchovies, then put in a mixing bowl with the egg, freshly ground spices, most of the herbs, and some lemon zest. Mix these altogether, then mash in the pork mince with your hand along with a teaspoon of salt. Divide the mixture up into 12 pieces, and pre-heat the oven to 170C / Fan 150 / Gas 3 / 325F.

In a heavy-bottomed or non-stick pan, heat some olive oil on a medium-high heat. Flatten the pork pieces a little between your palms and start frying them off. You'll likely have to do this in 2-3 batches. Once each side is coloured, transfer to an oven dish that will fit all 12 patties and allow for some liquid. Pour over the chicken stock – you only want them to be half-submerged, so use less if necessary, or top up with stock or water if you need more. Place in the oven to allow the patties to finish cooking – 10 minutes will be plenty.

While the pork's cooking, quarter the lettuces lengthways and give them a wash under running cold water.

Once the pork's cooked, divide the patties among 4 warmed plates, and break the lettuce up into the cooking liquor, seasoning with salt and pepper. Give it a stir around and return to the oven for 2 minutes to allow the lettuce to wilt down. Remove, pour over a good glug of olive oil, stir through the rest of the chopped herbs, and divide the lettuce and broth between the plates. If you have some in the fridge, a shaving of parmesan will top it off nicely.

Net carbs for whole recipe is 14.3g. For each serving, simply divide this weight by number of servings.

Lamb faggots with minted peas

Faggots are bundles of minced meat and liver. They're a great way of incorporating liver into your diet if you're not partial to the organ meat on its own. Feel free to try this with beef too, or even venison if you can get it at a good price. When basted with the stock they're cooking in, they come out the oven with a lovely golden gloss.

Serves 2 to 3

500g / 18oz lamb mince / ground lamb
200g / 7oz lamb liver
3 onions
4 cloves of garlic
A good pinch each of nutmeg, clove, white pepper and cinnamon, plus a bigger pinch of allspice
500ml / 2 cups chicken stock
4 handfuls of frozen peas
2 sprigs of mint, plus a small handful of leaves
EV olive oil or beef dripping

Slice up two of the onions and all of the garlic, and sweat them down in some olive oil or dripping on a low heat. Season with salt and pepper and keep going until they're very soft but without colour – around 15-20 minutes.
Preheat the oven to 220C / Fan 200 / Gas 7 / 425F.

While the onions and garlic are sweating down, finely dice the other onion and put it in a bowl with the lamb mince and the spices. Chop up the liver as finely as you can, add that to the bowl with 1 tsp of salt, and mix everything well with your hands. Shape into 4 balls.

Add the chicken stock and the mint sprigs into the garlic and onion mix, bring up to the boil, then remove from the heat and set aside. If the four faggots aren't likely to fit in this pan, transfer to a dish in which they will.

Place the meat in the onions and stock. If they're not submerged by a third, add a little more stock or water.

Place in the oven for around 25 minutes, basting a couple of times with the stock. They need to be cooked through, so keep squeezing them to see how they're coming along, and pierce one with a thin sharp knife or a skewer if you're unsure – the juice should not run any shade of red. The top should be golden and glossy. You can open one up to check the meat is not pink. If it is still a little pink, give it another five minutes.

Once they're cooked, pick out the mint and drop in the peas, and return to the oven for 2 minutes so that they heat through. Finally, chop up the fresh mint, stir through, and divide between bowls.

Net carbs for whole recipe is 47.3g. For each serving, simply divide this weight by number of servings.

NOSE-TO-TAIL:
SLOW-COOKING THE
CHEAPER CUTS

Beef short rib with mushrooms, spinach & tarragon
Lamb breast with cavolo nero, cherry tomatoes & tzatziki
Pork casserole
Braised lamb shoulder with spiced carrots, orange & mint
Beef rendang
Roast pork belly with two slaws

I'm at my happiest when revolving my life around something slow-cooked. I can both relax and concentrate so much easier when there's something braising away in the oven for a few hours. Cooking this way is transformative: you see inexpensive pieces of meat – tails, cheeks, bellies and necks – turn priceless, tender, and succulent over the course of an afternoon. It's always worth using bone-in cuts here, as it not only helps keep the meat moist, but contributes to the flavour of the liquid in the case of braising.

Beef short rib with mushrooms, spinach & tarragon

The greatest pleasure of cooking short rib – apart from the tender, fatty textures it gives you after a few hours in the oven – is in the browning. They come in layered cuboids of meat and fat, with a great rib bone running through them, and they take on a glorious golden colour when seared before braising. You'll know they're ready to eat when the bone slips away from the rest, and you may, like me, be sorry to throw it in the bin. Rather than giving a precise quantity for the short rib, I suggest you estimate by eye how much you'll need per person, bearing in mind that some pieces will have more bone than others. The best thing is to chat to your butcher about this.

Feeds 2

Enough short rib for 2 people (also known as Jacob's ladder or boiling beef)
200g / 7oz mushrooms, torn roughly into 2-3 pieces
1 small onion, roughly sliced
2 cloves of garlic
1 tsp mustard, Dijon or wholegrain
1 bay leaf
1 tsp dried thyme
4 stalks of fresh tarragon
500ml / 2 cups of chicken stock
150g / 1/3lb baby spinach, washed
Small glass of red wine (optional)
Wine vinegar (optional)

Preheat your oven to 150C / Fan 130 / Gas 2 / 300F. You'll need a casserole dish large enough to hold the beef and mushrooms plus their cooking liquor.

Salt your pieces of beef, then start browning them off in a hot pan with a drizzle of olive oil or some beef dripping if you have it. Give each side a good 3-4 minutes, or until it's nice and golden, then turn and repeat until the slabs of beef are coloured all over. You may have to do it in batches, and you'll find some fat rendering into the pan – if it becomes too much, just tip it out into a bowl and keep in the fridge for frying things another time.

When all the meat is browned, remove from the pan, turn the temperature down to medium, and tip out most of the fat. Fry the mushrooms first, and once the liquid they release has evaporated add the onions and garlic, seasoning with salt and pepper and some extra oil or dripping if the mushrooms have soaked up all the fat. Continue until the onions have softened and the mushrooms are looking a bit glossier – around 5 minutes.

Stir through the teaspoon of mustard and the thyme and allow to cook out for 2-3 minutes. If you have some wine lying around, add a small glass and allow to reduce by around half.

Combine the beef and vegetables in the dish you're going to cook them in. Tuck in the bay leaves and 2 stalks of the tarragon and pour over the chicken stock. The contents need to be only just submerged, so add a little more stock or water if the 500ml isn't quite enough. Give everything a nudge into place, and allow it to come to the boil.

Check the seasoning - the meat needs to braise in seasoned liquid, but do bear in mind that the liquid will reduce - then cover with a lid or tinfoil, and place in the oven for around 3 hours, or until the beef is starting to slip easily off the bones.

Once the meat is cooked, remove from the oven and check again for seasoning. A splash of wine vinegar will help to lift it, but the broth is also fine left rich and uncut. Divide the meat and the vegetables among 2 large bowls, then add the spinach to the broth.

Stir this through, and while it's wilting strip the leaves from the remaining tarragon stalks and distribute them between the serving bowls. When the spinach is wilted, divide this out too, before giving each bowl a good ladle or two of the delicious liquid.

Net carbs for whole recipe is 16.6g. For each serving, simply divide this weight by number of servings.

Lamb breast with cavolo nero, cherry tomatoes & tzatziki

Lamb breast is somewhat slighter than pork belly, but it's extremely filling, great value for money, and the perfect port of call if you're looking to increase your fat intake. The sweet cherry tomatoes and fresh tzatziki provide a foil to that here. Ask your butcher to take the meat off the bone for you (or buy it from the supermarket with no bones), but take the bones home to make a stock with, and once it's cooked feel free to remove the layer of white membrane, which some feel is too tough to eat.

Serves 2

450g / 1lb boneless lamb breast (sometimes called flank or belly)
1 large onion
150g / 1/3lb cherry tomatoes
3 cloves of garlic, skin on
2 large handfuls of cavolo nero leaves, stripped from their stalk
Around 100g / 3.5oz Greek-style or natural yogurt
¼ of a cucumber
A small handful of fresh mint leaves, chopped, or 1 tsp dried mint
A lemon

Pre-heat the oven to 200C / Fan 180 / Gas 6 / 400F.

Rub the lamb belly all over with a little olive oil and season with salt. Cut the onion into 1cm slices and add just enough olive oil to coat. Spread the onions in an oven dish in the shape of the lamb, then place the lamb itself on top, and roast in the oven for 20-30 minutes or until the meat is browned. Add 200ml of water, turn the temperature down to 140C, and give it another 2-2½ hours.

When that time's nearly up, start preparing your other components.

Put a pot of water onto boil for the cavolo nero. Meantime, place the cherry tomatoes and garlic cloves on a small oven tray. Season with salt and pepper, drizzle with olive oil, and roast in the same oven as the lamb for around 15-20 minutes, or just until the skins are starting to burst a little.

To make the tzatziki, split the cucumber lengthwise and use a teaspoon to scrape out the watery core. Grate the two halves coarsely and place in a bowl with a little salt mixed through. Leave this to sit for 10 minutes, then use your hands to squeeze as much water as you can from the grated cucumber. Place the remains in a bowl and stir enough yogurt to give you the kind of consistency you'd like. Stir through the mint and check for seasoning.

Once the water's boiling, season with salt and blanch the greens for 2 minutes. If you prefer it with less bite, cook for longer. Strain over a colander once cooked to your satisfaction.

Check the lamb by pulling at a rib bone. If it's starting to come away easily from the meat then it's ready, otherwise give it a little longer. Allow it to rest for 10 minutes once you've removed it from the oven.

To serve, divide the lamb into two portions in whatever way you like. Reheat the cavolo nero in the oven dish so that it soaks up the lamb juices and fat, then add a squeeze of lemon juice. Place a portion of lamb on top, and drop a few cherry tomatoes around it. Add a dollop of tzatziki, and drizzle it all with any juices that remain in the oven dishes in which you cooked the tomatoes and lamb. Scatter over some fresh mint leaves if you have any left.

Net carbs for whole recipe is 36.9g. For each serving, simply divide this weight by number of servings.

Pork casserole

It's traditional to brown meat before braising it, as the colouring contributes lots of flavour to the liquid it cooks in. But there's a humble elegance about taking a gentler approach, and for me pork somehow encourages it more than other meats. It also makes this an easy one-pot wonder.

Serves 2

350g / 12.5oz diced pork shoulder
2 carrots
1 medium onion
1 head of fennel
1 bulb of garlic
A bunch of hard herbs – thyme, rosemary and/or bay – tied up with some string
500ml / 2 cups chicken stock
Lots of fresh parsley

Set the oven to 150C / Fan 130 / Gas 2 / 300F. You'll need an oven-proof casserole dish that fits everything snugly.

Peel and halve the onion and cut into thick slices. Trim the discoloured bottom of the fennel, and slice it in the same way. Add both to the pot, along with the peeled carrots (leave them whole).

Trim the top end off the garlic just in order to expose the cloves, and pop this in too, along with the herbs.

Add the pork shoulder, season everything with salt and pepper, and toss around to distribute.
Pour over the chicken stock. If it doesn't quite cover the contents, add some more stock or some water. If you have some lying around, include a small glass of white wine.

Bring the pot to the boil, skimming off and discarding any scum that rises to the surface with a ladle.

Place the lid on and transfer to the oven for 2 hours. By this point the pork should be nice and tender, but if you feel it needs longer then continue cooking.

Once it's ready, remove from the oven and allow to rest for half an hour. When it's cool enough to handle, remove the garlic bulb and squeeze the cloves back into the pot. Stir through the chopped parsley, chop up the carrots, and share between two deep plates.

Net carbs for whole recipe is 34.2g.
For each serving, simply divide this
weight by number of servings.

Braised lamb shoulder with spiced carrots, orange & mint

Lamb shoulder is my desert island meat. If you're feeding a few people it's worth buying the whole limb, but a butcher will cut you off a part if you ask, and supermarkets often stock pieces of varying sizes. If you can't get a single piece on the bone, diced shoulder meat is absolutely fine.

Feeds 2

450g / 1lb lamb shoulder, preferably bone-in
1 bulb of garlic
2 small onions
3 tsp cumin seeds
4 sprigs of fresh mint, or 2 tsp dried mint
A lemon
600ml / 2.5 cups chicken or lamb stock
4 large carrots, or 6 smaller ones
1 orange
1 tsp ground cinnamon
1 tsp ground coriander
1½ tbsp honey
A small handful of fresh herbs, such as parsley, coriander or mint
Yogurt (optional)

Set the oven to 150C / Fan 130 / Gas 2 / 300F. You'll need an oven-proof casserole dish that fits everything snugly.

Season the lamb all over, then brown it on all sides in some olive oil or beef dripping on a medium heat.

Meantime peel and thickly slice the onions, and trim the top off the garlic so that you just expose the cloves inside. Set aside 2 cloves, but leave the rest intact.

Once the meat's nicely coloured, remove it from the pan and add the onions and garlic bulb, along with 2 teaspoons of the cumin seeds. Season and allow to sweat down for 5-10 minutes, stirring in order to scrape any fragments of lamb off the bottom of the pan. Nestle the mint sprigs among the vegetables (or add the dried mint), pop in 2 strips of the lemon rind, and return the shoulder to the pot.

Now pour in the chicken stock and bring it to the boil. The lamb should be only just submerged in the liquid, so add more stock or water if it's not quite enough. Check the seasoning - the meat needs to braise in seasoned liquid, but do bear in mind that the liquid will reduce - then cover with a lid or tinfoil, and braise in the oven for 2½-3 hours.

While the lamb's in the oven, prepare the carrots for roasting.

Peel the carrots and quarter them lengthwise. If they're particularly long, chop them in half first. Place them in a bowl with all the spices (including the remaining teaspoon of cumin), add a good glug of olive oil, season with salt, and toss everything around so the carrots are well coated.

Spread over a lined baking tray.
Halve the orange, and put one half to the side. Cut the other in half again, then slice thinly into little quarter discs, around 2-3mm thick, and set aside too.
Once the lamb's out the oven, allow the meat to rest for half an hour, turn the oven up to 200 degrees, and roast the carrots for 15 minutes.

Once this time's up, remove the tray from the oven, add the orange slices and the honey, mix everything together, and return to the oven for another 15-20 minutes, tossing again half way through. After that, check to see that the carrots are cooked – you'll be able to slip the tip of a knife into the thickest part with no trouble. By this point, the oranges and honey will also have caramelised a little.

Remove from the oven, squeeze over the juice of the other orange half, and toss through the fresh herbs.

The lamb should now have cooled enough for you to remove and discard the mint sprigs, and to squeeze out the garlic cloves from the bulb and mash into the liquid.

To serve, distribute the carrots and the lamb with its juices among deep plates. Finish with some finely shredded mint leaves if you have any left, and a dollop of yogurt will bring the two components together nicely.

Net carbs for whole recipe is 85.5g. For each serving, simply divide this weight by number of servings. You can cut the carbs on this dish considerably by just making the lamb part and combining with another side dish.

Beef rendang

In 2018, Paleo Canteen served up rendang from our stall at a music festival. Saturday was so busy that we had to cook all night to make more for the morning, and by Sunday night we'd sold out again. You don't have to cook your rendang overnight, but hopefully it will be as popular as ours was. There are quite a few ingredients here, but most of them are spices that can be in your cupboard already. Traditionally this is a dry curry dish, so don't be alarmed if you end up without too much sauce. Use any stewing cut of beef here - brisket, shin, chuck, or cheek are all good options.

Serves 2-3

Coconut oil
450g / 1lb stewing beef, diced
2 tbsp desiccated coconut
3 banana shallots, peeled
6 cloves garlic, peeled
1 inch of ginger, sliced thinly against the grain
3 sticks of lemongrass, sliced thinly
2 red chillies, sliced
½ tsp ground cinnamon
¾ tsp ground turmeric
2 whole star anise
3 cardamom pods
1 tin full fat coconut milk (400ml / 1.75 cups)
A lime, zested and juiced
Some fresh coriander

Preheat the oven to 160C / Fan 140 / gas mark 2-3 / 310F. You'll need an oven-proof casserole dish that fits everything snugly.

Brown off the meat in coconut oil or beef dripping on a medium-high heat, until it's well coloured all over.

Toast the desiccated coconut in a dry pan, tossing it regularly until golden all over, then set aside.

While this is happening, make a paste by blitzing together in a food processor the shallots, garlic, ginger, lemongrass and chillies. If you like it spicy, keep the chilli seeds. If you prefer it mild, discard the seeds. Add a tablespoon or two of water if needed, just to loosen it up.

Once the beef is browned, remove from the pan, and tip out the fat if it's looking a bit dark. Add a little more coconut oil if so, and gently toast the cinnamon, turmeric, star anise and cardamom for a minute to let them release their aromas. Now add the paste, season with salt, and cook everything out for 3 minutes on a low heat.

Next add the toasted coconut and the coconut milk, allowing any fatty chunks to dissolve before returning the beef to the pan and bringing everything up to the boil. The meat should be only just submerged, so add water to top up the coconut milk if necessary. Cover and place in the preheated oven for 2½ hours. After 1½ hours, give it a stir and add 100ml of water if it's starting to stick to the pot. It's ready when the meat is tender. If it's still quite liquidy by the time the meat is cooked, remove the meat and allow the sauce to reduce on the stove.

Check the seasoning, and serve with the lime juice and zest stirred in, and some fresh coriander.

Net carbs for whole recipe is 23.3g. For each serving, simply divide this weight by number of servings.

Roast pork belly with two slaws

Pork belly is one of the great cheap cuts. The layers of fat between layers of meat keep it extra moist while cooking, and the contrast with the golden, crispy crackling on top makes it a real treat despite its apparent devaluation. I think it works best with something fresh and crunchy on the side, so two alternative slaw salads follow the instructions for cooking the pork itself.

Serves 3-4

1kg / 2lb4oz slab of pork belly, bone-in, skin on
1 tsp fennel seeds, freshly ground
1 tsp black pepper, freshly ground
1 large onion
1 bulb of garlic
2 bay leaves
Half a lemon

The important thing to consider when roasting pork belly is that it needs a long time on a low temperature in order to tenderise the meat, as well as a shorter blast at a high temperature in order to crisp up the crackling. I start with the blast, then turn it down (though I've seen it done the other way around

to good effect). It's something you'll have to play around with, depending largely on how your oven works.

Pre-heat your oven to 220C / Fan 200 / Gas 7 / 425F. Lay the pork skin-side up and run the tip of your knife across the skin in close parallel lines, working your way from one side to the other. You want to score the surface, not penetrate the skin into the fat, so don't put too much pressure on it. Now flip the belly so that it's skin-side down, rub with a little oil, and season well with salt, followed by the fennel and pepper.

Peel and thickly slice the onion, then place it on the bottom of the oven tray on which you'll cook your pork. Break the garlic bulb into cloves, rip up the bay leaves, and add these to the onions. Toss everything in a little olive oil or beef dripping, lay out in the shape of the belly, and place the pork on top.

Now rub the lemon half all over the pork skin, squeezing gently as you go, so as to coat it in a little juice. Season liberally with salt, and place in the hot oven.

You're now waiting for the crackling to form, which should take around 30 minutes (turn the tray round halfway through). If you keep an eye on it, you'll see it appearing gradually across the surface. If the whole skin isn't covered after 30 minutes, just give it longer, it'll get there. On the other hand, if it looks as though it's getting a little too dark in the process, turn your oven down slightly. Once a hardened, bubbly layer has formed, remove from the oven, and add enough water to create a 1cm layer of liquid (do not pour it over the skin!).

Return the pork to the oven and turn the heat down to 150. It'll need 3 hours minus the amount of time it's already been in. Keep an eye on it throughout this time though, as you may need to add more water to prevent the onions from burning.

Once the time's up, remove from the oven and allow to rest for half an hour before eating. If you feel that the skin could be more crackled, place it under a medium hot grill until you're happy with it (be careful, it can happen quickly).

Before serving, remove the rib bones from underneath, then carve off slices with a serrated knife. The bones can be used to make a light pork stock for another meal.

Savoy slaw

Quarter of a savoy cabbage
2 carrots
2 red onions
1 big handful of fresh parsley
4 heaped tbsp of mayonnaise (see p.160)
Wine vinegar
Half a lemon

Remove and discard the outer leaf of the savoy cabbage and any thick stalk. Peel off the layers of leaves and wash them well in a basin of cold water. Rinse off and slice as finely as you can, then place in a bowl, season well with salt, and set aside for 1 hour. In the meantime, peel and julienne or grate the carrots, and finely slice the onions. Once the hour's up, squeeze handfuls of the cabbage to remove any excess moisture. If it tastes too salty, give it a quick rinse. Place it in a bowl with the carrot and onion, and stir through the mayonnaise plus a squeeze of the lemon juice. Now add a dash of vinegar, and check the flavour: if you prefer it looser, add more mayo; if you prefer it sharper, more vinegar. Lastly stir through the freshly chopped parsley.

Asian hot slaw

Quarter of a white cabbage
4 big leaves of spring greens
2 red chillies
1 clove of garlic
4 spring onions
½ tsp Chinese 5 spice
2 tbsp light olive oil
2 tsp sesame oil
A lime
Rice wine vinegar or white wine
vinegar
1 big handful of fresh coriander

Put a small pot of water on to boil. Remove and discard the outer leaf of the white cabbage and any thick stalk , then slice the leaves as finely as you can, place in a bowl and season well with salt, and set aside for 1 hour.

Remove the leaf from the stalk of the spring greens, roll up tightly in a tube, and slice as finely as you can. Once the water's boiling, salt it, and blanch the greens for 1 minutes. Strain and rinse in plenty of cold water.

Peel and crush the garlic, finely slice the chilli and spring onions on an angle, and place in a bowl. Lightly toast the 5 spice on a low, dry heat for 20 seconds, and add this to the bowl too along with the oils and half

a teaspoon of salt. Give it all a stir through and set aside.

Once the hour's up, squeeze handfuls of the white cabbage to remove any excess moisture, and do the same with the greens. Add both to the bowl, along with the juice and zest of the lime, a teaspoon of vinegar, and the fresh coriander. Mix well, and check the seasoning, adjusting to your own taste.

Net carbs for whole recipe is 18.5g for the pork, 32.3g for the savoy slaw, and 17.7g for the Asian slaw. For each serving, simply divide thie total weight by number of servings.

Chicken thighs with green beans, courgette ribbons and pesto
Sausages with pepperonata
Roast chicken with carrots, greens and gravy
Pork shoulder steaks with spinach and lemon
Steak three ways
Chicken shawarma with chopped salad and garlic yogurt

There's not always time to cook things low and slow, and some cuts of meat are made to be cooked quickly on a higher heat. A budget might mean foregoing some of the classic roasting joints – beef sirloin, leg of lamb, venison haunch – but there's no shortage of other options. Most of the dishes that follow – roast chicken being the exception – are perfect for a barbeque, so keep these in mind for warmer months.

Chicken thighs with green beans, courgette ribbons & pesto

Chicken thighs have to be the best part of the bird: tender, tasty, and suitable for both slow-braising and fast-roasting. They also take on marinades and retain their juiciness better than the breast. Remember to keep the thigh bones once you've finished as they'll provide you with a light stock to enhance another meal.

Feeds 2

4 chicken thighs, skin-on
2 garlic cloves, skin left on and bashed with the back of a knife
1 bay leaf
160g / 1/3lb green beans, topped but not tailed
Half a courgette / zucchini
1 jar of pesto (or make your own: see p.160)
A lemon
1 tbsp of butter

Pre-heat the oven to 160C / Fan 140 / Gas 2-3 / 310F. You'll need a pan that's oven-proof and which fits 4 thighs snugly.

Place your pan on a medium-high heat and add a drizzle of olive oil. Season the chicken thighs all over with salt, and place them skin-side-down in the pan. Allow them to colour without moving them around too much, turning them once each side is nice and golden.

Once they're coloured, turn the thighs skin-side-up and tip the fat out into a small bowl or cup. Add the garlic cloves and bay leaf, and pour over enough water so that a layer of water comes around a third of the way up the thighs. Put the pan in the oven uncovered and leave to gently roast for 45-50 minutes.

Bring a pan of water to the boil, season with salt, and cook the green beans. Drain them after 2 minutes, and return the pot to the heat. Add the fat that you poured off when searing the chicken thighs, and tip in the green beans along with a good grinding of black pepper.

On a low-medium heat, allow the beans to cook for a further 15 minutes, tossing around now and then, during which time they'll soften, sweeten, and take on the flavour of the chicken fat.

While this is going on, use a peeler to take long strips off the courgette, and leave these aside until everything else is good to go.

When the chicken is cooked, remove the thighs onto a warm plate, and return the pot with the liquid, garlic and bay leaf to a high heat. Allow it to reduce down so that you're left with a few tablespoons of chicken sauce. Whisk in a tablespoon of cold butter at the end, to give it some gloss and richness.

To serve, fold the courgette ribbons through the green beans, along with a tablespoon of pesto (or more, or less, depending on your taste). Add a squeeze of lemon juice to lift it a little, and a pinch of salt if it needs it. Place a mound of this onto each plate, top with two thighs, and drizzle the pan juices around everything.

Net carbs for whole recipe is 19g. For each serving, simply divide this weight by number of servings.

Roast chicken with carrots, greens & gravy

This is somewhere between a roast and a pot-roast, where resting the bird with the lid on after roasting helps produce the most delicious juices for cooking your vegetables in. Buy an appropriately sized chicken for the number of people you wish to feed, and take note of its weight before disposing of the packet so that you know how long to cook it for.

1 whole chicken
1 bulb of garlic
Half a lemon
100g / 3.5oz butter
A few sprigs of thyme
Enough carrots and spring greens (or similar) for however many you're feeding

You'll need a dish that fits the chicken snugly – an oval casserole dish with a lid is ideal.
Set the oven to its highest setting and put a pot of water on to boil.

Leaving the chicken trussed (if it came like that), rub it all over with a little olive oil, then season all over with salt. Trim the top off the garlic bulb in order to just expose the cloves, then pop this in the cavity along with the butter, thyme and half lemon. Sit the chicken in the pot and put in the hot oven for 20 minutes, allowing it to colour well.

Peel the carrots and slice into 1cm rounds. Prepare the greens by washing them and stripping away any stalks that are particularly thick or tough, then roll up the leaves and cut them into nice thick ribbons.

When the time's up on the chicken, remove from the oven and baste it with the buttery juices that have gathered in the pot. If it's easier than getting your spoon in, just carefully pour all the juices into a bowl and then pour them back over the chicken. Return to the oven, turn the temperature down to 140C / Fan 120 / Gas 1 / 275F, and give it another 40 minutes per kilo (so that a 1.5kg chicken, for instance, will require
an additional hour).

Add plenty of salt to the boiling water and blanch the carrots for

3 minutes. Remove to a colander and blanch the greens for the same amount of time. Remove to the colander, run some cold water over both, then leave to drip dry in the colander.

When the time's up on your chicken, remove from the oven, undo the trussing, and check that the juices run clear when you cut into a thick part of the thigh. If they don't, continue cooking for another 10 minutes before checking again. When it's cooked, baste a few times with the juices again then cover with a lid or tinfoil and sit away from the heat for 1 hour.

After the hour, remove the chicken to a plate and put the pot with all the juice on a low-medium heat on the stove. Dig out the garlic bulb from the bird and squeeze out the cloves, mushing them in the pan. Add the carrots to this and allow them took until they're nice and soft.

Lastly, stir through the greens and give them a few minutes to re-heat and take on some juice.

To serve, carve up the chicken and share with the vegetables among deep plates. Top with lots of the pan juice. If you have some aioli in the fridge, add a big dollop of that too.

Net carbs for whole recipe is 24.8g. For each serving, simply divide this weight by number of servings.

Pork shoulder steaks with spinach & lemon

You can often buy pork shoulder cut into steaks at the supermarket at a good price. If you don't feel like dicing and slow-braising them, this is a good and relatively quick alternative.

Serves 2

1-2 pork shoulder steaks per person
A lemon
4 cloves of garlic
½ tsp fennel seeds, crushed
½ tsp cracked black pepper
½ tsp chilli flakes
2 sprigs of rosemary or thyme, or 2 bay leaves
4 big handfuls of baby spinach, washed

Mix the garlic, fennel seeds, black pepper and chilli flakes with 1 teaspoon of salt. Chop up the rosemary or thyme, or else tear up the bay leaves, mix this into the spices, then add enough olive oil to be able to rub the marinade all over the steaks. Set aside for half an hour at room temperature.

Heat a non-stick or heavy-bottomed pan on medium-high. Give the steaks another rub around, then add a drizzle of olive oil to the pan and start frying them. Allow them to colour nicely before flipping. Depending on their thickness, they'll need around 5 minutes on each side – turn the heat down if it looks as though they're colouring too fast.

Once cooked, remove them from the pan and let them rest on a warmed plate.

On a medium heat, add the spinach and a scant amount of water to the pan to create some steam. Allow the spinach to wilt down, scraping the bottom of the pan to get the flavour from the pork.

Once it's cooked, season with salt and pepper, squeeze against the side of the pan, and sit atop the pork steaks. Douse it all with a good squeeze of lemon juice.

Net carbs for whole recipe is 24.6g. For each serving, simply divide this weight by number of servings.

Sausages with pepperonata

The trinity of pork, peppers and fennel seed really makes my mouth water, and this is a fairly quick and easy rendition of it. Try to buy sausages with as high a percentage of pork as possible.

Feeds 2

2-3 sausages per person
3 peppers, whatever combination
of red and yellow you like
4 cloves of garlic
1 tsp fennel seeds, crushed
½ tsp cracked black pepper
½ tsp dried chilli flakes
Red or white wine vinegar

Start with the pepperonata, which you want to cook slowly over 30-45 minutes.

Halve and de-seed the peppers, then cut lengthwise into 1cm slices. Place a pan on a medium heat and add a generous few glugs of olive oil. Fry the garlic for half a minute, making sure not to allow it to colour, then add the peppers, fennel seed, black pepper and dried chillies, and season with salt. Give everything a good toss around, then cover, turn down low, and leave to cook for around half an hour, removing the lid every 5 minutes or so in order to stir and ensure that nothing is sticking. You don't want any colour on the peppers – the idea is to stew them down and allow their natural sweetness to come out, rather than to caramelise them. Once you're happy with how soft they are, check for salt, add a dash of vinegar, and remove from the heat. They should be silky and sweet and oily.

Now it's just a case of cooking your sausages. Fry them in a little olive oil on a medium heat. Placing a lid on top helps give them a gloss, as the steam condenses, drips down, and emulsifies with the fat. You can of course also grill them if you prefer. The important thing is not to prick them, and not to overcook them, as they'll lose some of their fat one way and much of their moisture the other.

To serve, place a portion of pepperonata on a plate and top with the sausages.

Net carbs for whole recipe is 33.9g. For each serving, simply divide this weight by number of servings.

Steak three ways

Popular cuts of beef like ribeye, sirloin and fillet hardly fit the low-budget bill, but there are plenty of other cuts out there that come in much more affordable, like featherblade (or flat-iron), bavette (sometimes called thin flank) and onglet (skirting, hanger steak). These might lack the marbled quality of a ribeye or the tenderness of a fillet, but they can be every bit as tasty, and an excellent ruminant source of fat and nutrients. They also rank high in terms of bang for buck, as they're likely to leave you feeling sated for a long time. This recipe gives some tips on cooking your steak, followed by my three go-to garnishes.

Cooking steak:

This will of course depend on the cut you're using and how thick it is, along with your preferred cooking degree. But some constants in this are:
Use a cast-iron or heavy-bottomed pan on a high heat to sear you steak, with the aim of getting as much colour in a short amount of time as you can. If you're using a thin cut, this is all the more important, as it's likely to cook all the way in the pan. Slip a small knob of butter in with the steak to help with the colouring, otherwise a drizzle of light olive oil or, ideally, some beef dripping, is fine for this stage.

Keep moving the steak around the hot pan until it's all coloured, trying to maintain the sizzle sound.

If your steak is on the thicker side, you're best to transfer it to the oven to finish cooking once it's been browned in the pan. So before you start cooking it, pre-heat the oven with a tray inside to 150 degrees. Place the steak on the tray and give it however much more time you think it needs.

Judging cooking degree is a matter of practice and preference. Keep checking it with your fingers throughout cooking, both pressing it on the top and squeezing it from the sides, and imagine the spectrum of tenderness running from raw (very soft) to thoroughly cooked (very little give).
Always let your steak rest after cooking it – pre-heat a plate for this, and leave it for 10 minutes before slicing in.

Garnishes (all for 2 people):

Grilled romaine lettuce and quick green sauce

You can use other lettuces for this, such as baby gem or radicchio.

1 head of romaine lettuce
1 big handful of fresh parsley (plus some mint and/or basil if you have them)
1 tsp of capers
2 anchovies
1 clove of garlic
1 tsp Dijon mustard
Wine vinegar
A lemon

Heat a griddle or cast-iron pan on a high heat until smoking. Quarter the romaine lettuce lengthwise, brush the cut sides with olive oil, and place oil-side down in the pan. Leave until well coloured then turn onto the other cut side for the same amount of time. Once it's cooked, remove to a plate and dress with olive oil, salt and a squeeze of lemon juice.

For the green sauce, smash up the garlic and anchovies in a pestle and mortar. Roughly chop up the capers and add them, then stir through the mustard, a teaspoon of vinegar and a squeeze of lemon juice. Chop the parsley up finely (along with the other herbs if you have them), and stir through the rest. Taste for seasoning – salt and pepper, and some adjustments to the acidity according to your taste.

To serve, place the grilled lettuce on a plate, spread slices of the steak over the top, and drizzle with the green sauce as well as any steak juices that have collected during its rest.

Garlic mushrooms with tarragon butter sauce

2 Portobello mushrooms per person, or 4-5 each of regular mushrooms
100g / 3.5oz butter
4 cloves of garlic
1 banana shallot
4 sprigs of tarragon
White wine or sherry vinegar

Sit the mushrooms upside down in a roasting dish. Season with salt and pepper, crush 3 of the garlic cloves and distribute among the mushrooms, then use half the butter to do the same. Roast on 180 degrees for 10 minutes, then baste in the juices and return to the oven for another 5 minutes, or until cooked.

Put a small pan on a low-medium

heat, add a drizzle of olive oil and the rest of the butter. Finely dice the shallot and remaining garlic clove and sweat these down with salt and pepper until soft but without colour. When that's done, strip the tarragon leaves from the stalk and chop up, then stir this through and remove the pan from the heat.

When the mushrooms are cooked, pour all the juices from the oven dish into the tarragon butter. Once your steak is cooked, pour the resting juices in there too, and check for seasoning – a dash of vinegar will give it a little lift.

To serve, sit the mushrooms on top of the steak and pour over the sauce.

Roast tomatoes and parmesan

3 ripe tomatoes
Dried oregano
Parmesan, or similar hard cheese

Halve the tomatoes across the middle. Brush with olive oil, season with salt and pepper, sprinkle over some oregano, and roast in the oven on 140 degrees for around 30-45 minutes, or until they're cooked and starting to shrivel a little around the edges.

To serve, grate the cheese over the sliced steak and sit the tomatoes on the side.

Net carbs for whole recipe is 14.7g for the romaine lettuce side, 15g for the garlic mushrooms, and 10g for the roast tomatoes. For each serving, simply divide this weight by number of servings.

Chicken shawarma with chopped salad & garlic yogurt

The contents of a kebab are every bit as tasty without the flatbread wrapping, though they're better suited to a plate than eaten on the move. If lamb leg steaks are ever on offer, try this recipe with them too.

Serves 2

4 chicken thighs, boneless, skin on
5 cloves of garlic
1 tsp ground cumin
½ tsp cracked black pepper
¼ tsp turmeric
¼ tsp ground cardamom
¼ tsp ground cinnamon
¼ tsp ground nutmeg
¼ tsp cayenne pepper
1/3 of a cucumber
1 small red onion
A small handful of fresh dill
1 tsp sumac
150g / 1/3lb full-fat Greek-style yogurt
2 tbsp tahini
A lemon
Olive oil

Peel 4 of the 5 garlic cloves and put them in a pestle and mortar with all the spices and 1 tbsp of olive oil.

Pound everything together until you have a smooth paste, then drizzle in enough olive oil to make a suitable marinade consistency. Rub this all over the chicken thighs in a bowl, then add a squeeze of lemon juice and season well with salt. Cover, refrigerate, and leave to do its thing for at least 2 hours, or preferably overnight.

Grill the chicken thighs on a medium-high heat, trying to ensure a nice even colouring on each side. If they colour too quickly before they're cooked inside, just turn the heat down a little, and/or lower the grill tray away from the heat source.

While the chicken's cooking, dice up the cucumber, peel and finely slice the red onion, and toss together in a bowl with the sumac, freshly chopped dill and a drizzle of olive oil. Season with salt, a scraping of lemon zest, and a squeeze of lemon juice.

For the yogurt sauce, crush the remaining clove of garlic and put it in a bowl with the yogurt, tahini, squeeze of lemon juice, and 1 tbsp of olive oil. Stir everything together and adjust the seasoning to your taste. If you'd prefer the sauce a little thinner, simply add a touch of water (1 teaspoon at a time), or indeed some more lemon juice if you think it needs the acidity.

To serve, divide the chicken and salad between 2 plates, and help yourselves to sauce.

Net carbs for whole recipe is 17.2g. For each serving, simply divide this weight by number of servings.

Lamb liver with bacon, celeriac mash and caper butter
Ox tongue with braised red cabbage and horseradish
Lamb heart with fennel three ways
Devilled chicken livers
Ox liver with mixed alliums
Liver pâté

Organ meat is one of the most nutritionally dense foods available to us, yet for many people it remains an obstacle. Its flavour is certainly stronger than the usual muscle cuts, and its texture often a little different. We hope these recipes provide some reasons to embrace rather than shy away from these features of offal though, which is widely available and very inexpensive.

Lamb liver with bacon, celeriac mash & caper butter

If you're sold on the nutritional value of liver but on the fence about eating it, it's worth trying it cooked correctly – while it develops a grainy texture when overcooked, when left a little pink it retains a very appealing tenderness. Pairing it with bacon is classic, as the latter's fattiness really compliments the leanness of organ meat. This is a rich and warming dish that's perfect on a cold day.

Serves 2

400g / 14oz lamb liver
6 rashers streaky bacon, smoked or unsmoked
Half a celeriac / celery root
2 tbsp of capers, drained of brine
Butter
1 handful of fresh parsley, chopped
A lemon

Scrub the celeriac well under a running tap, then peel it. Remove any awkward knobbly bits with a knife. Cut it into even dices and place in a pot, cover with water and season with salt, and bring to the boil. Turn down to a simmer and cook until you can pierce them

easily with a knife – around 15 minutes, depending on what size you cut them to. Drain, allow to drip dry for 5 minutes, then mash in a big spoonful of butter and season with salt and pepper to taste. Set aside with a lid on while you cook the rest.

Put a non-stick or heavy-bottomed frying pan on a high heat for the liver. If your pan isn't large enough for all the liver, be prepared to cook it in two rounds. The trick with liver is to get colour on the outside without overcooking it on the inside: this gives it flavour whilst avoiding the grainy texture that many people find unpleasant about it.

Once the pan's nice and hot, add a drizzle of olive oil and a spoonful of butter, then place the livers in. Give them around 2 minutes on each side, shifting them around now and then.

Remove the livers onto a warm plate, tip the fat out of the pan, return to a medium heat, and fry the bacon rashers to your liking with a little olive oil. Add these to the livers once they're cooked, return the pan again to a medium heat, and add 2 tablespoons of butter along with the capers. Allow it all to melt and come to a foam, then immediately remove from the heat and add the parsley along with a squeeze of lemon juice.

To serve, check that the celeriac is still warm enough – if it's not, give it a quick reheat on the stove – and divide it in dollops among plates. Top with the livers – slice them up first if you prefer – the bacon, and lastly a couple of spoonfuls of the caper and parsley butter.

Net carbs for whole recipe is 24.1g. For each serving, simply divide this weight by number of servings.

Ox tongue with braised red cabbage & horseradish

An ox tongue goes a long way. If you don't like it sliced up for cold cuts, cut it nice and thick and chargrill it – it may well change your perception of this delicious cut of beef. Ask your butcher for a 'pickled' one, which means it's been brined and will have much better flavour and texture. You're best to work a day ahead with this so that the tongue has plenty of time to cool, but you could also slice and serve it up freshly braised.

Serves plenty

1 ox tongue, brined or 'pickled'
2 bay leaves
1 onion, peeled and halved
1 tsp black peppercorns
4 cloves
A quarter of a red cabbage
Red wine vinegar
Some honey
1 jar of horseradish cream

Pre-heat the oven to 150C / Fan 130 / Gas 2 / 300F. Place the tongue in a pan in which it fits snugly, add the bay leaves, onion, peppercorns and cloves, pour over enough water to just cover everything, and bring up to the boil with a lid on. Once it's boiling, put it in the oven for 2½ hours. When the time's up, check how easy it is to pierce the tongue with a small, sharp knife – if it slots in without much resistance it's ready, but if you feel you have to stab it a bit, then give it another half an hour. Bear in mind it will continue to cook a little when it's out the oven and resting in the liquid.

When it's ready, remove from the oven and allow to cool with the lid off for at least an hour, or until it's cool enough to handle. Tongues have a skin on them, which it's important to peel off while it's still warm (it's harder to do when it's cold). Once peeled, allow to cool further, then clingfilm and refrigerate.

For the cabbage, remove the outer leaf and the core, then slice it up thinly and place in a pot with a big ladle of the tongue liquor and 50ml of red wine vinegar. Season with salt and pepper, then cook down on a low-medium heat until the cabbage is softened and much of the liquor reduced. If it starts to look dry at any point, add some more of the tongue liquor. Once you're happy with how it's cooked, check for seasoning: if you like this kind of thing sharp, add some more vinegar; if you find it already a little tart, stir through a small amount of honey to balance it out.

Put a griddle pan on high heat and let it get smoking. Slice up the cold tongue to a thickness of around 1½cm – you'll want a couple of slices per person. Brush with olive oil, then start to sear on the pan, turning each side 90 degrees after a couple of minutes to get crossbar marks. Once that side's nicely marked, turn over and repeat. They should take around 3 minutes on each side.

To serve, place the griddled tongue and red cabbage on a plate along with a dollop of horseradish cream.

The tongue will last in the fridge for up to 5 days. Be sure to keep the stock, as it's gelatinous and full of flavour.

Net carbs for whole recipe is 25.8g. For each serving, simply divide this weight by number of servings.

Lamb heart with fennel three ways

If you're hesitant about offal, heart is a good place to start. Its texture and taste are not as challenging as organs like kidney or liver, and it's also more versatile. This dish makes a great starter, and is perfect for a BBQ in the summertime. There's a bit of preparation involved, so set aside some time so you can take pleasure in it.

Serves 2

4 lamb hearts
1½ tsp dried oregano
½ tsp fennel seeds, freshly ground
½ tsp chilli flakes
3 cloves of garlic, skinned and minced
2 garlic cloves, skinned and bashed
A lemon
Olive oil
2 heads of fennel

Start by preparing the lamb, so that it has time to marinade. Cut the lamb hearts so that you can spread them out flat on a board, inside up. Remove the veiny strands in thin layers with a sharp knife, so that you're left with a reasonably uniform strip comprised of dark lean and white fat. Go easy on trimming off the fat. Transfer them to a bowl and season well with salt and pepper.

In another bowl, make your marinade by mixing together the oregano, ground fennel seed, chilli flakes, and the minced garlic. Add a squeeze of lemon juice and a few good glugs of olive oil in order to make a dressing that will coat the hearts. Rub a couple of tablespoons of the marinade into the lamb hearts, and set aside in the fridge. Zest the lemon and add this to the remainder of the marinade, which you'll use to dress the fennel.

Put a griddle pan on a high heat, and start preparing the fennel. Trim off the green stalks and set aside, then stand the fennel up on your board, trim off the two ends, and set these aside too. Cut the fennel down the way into nice oval sections around half a centimetre thick, and brush them with olive oil. When the pan's hot enough, start grilling them, turning them over when you're happy with the char marks.

Once they're nicely coloured and

cooked – they'll take around 3 minutes on each side – transfer them to the bowl with the marinade in it and coat them all over. Check for seasoning, and leave the griddle pan on high.

Take the green fennel stalks that you trimmed off, slice these into rounds as thinly as possible, and add them to the marinade too. Set aside to let the flavours mingle.

Take the remainder of the fennel trim and dice it up finely. Place in a small pan with some olive oil and the two bashed garlic cloves, season with salt, and sauté on a low heat until it softens enough to mash with a fork. This is simply a way of both using up all the fennel and adding another texture to the dish.

Now start grilling the lamb hearts on the hot pan, again turning them when they're nicely marked. Heart is nice with a little pink inside, so be careful not to overcook them. Once cooked, slice on the angle and squeeze over some lemon juice.
To serve, divide the mashed fennel between two plates, set the grilled fennel on top of this, and lay the strips of heart by their side. Finish off by drizzling the fennel stalks and marinade mix over everything.

Net carbs for whole recipe is 39.8g. For each serving, simply divide this weight by number of servings.

Devilled chicken livers

Chicken livers are virtually synonymous with pate, but they're fantastic fried up on their own. They have a lovely tender texture when left rosy inside, and they hold their own when paired with other robust flavours like here. You can easily find them frozen in supermarkets, as well as from many fishmongers. If you're buying frozen, allow them to defrost before cooking.

Serves 2

200g / 7oz chicken livers
1 banana shallot, or 2 small round ones
1 red chilli
2 cloves of garlic
1 tsp Dijon mustard
¼ tsp cayenne pepper
¼ tsp ground cumin
1 bay leaf, halved
75ml / 1/3 cup double cream / heavy whipping cream
50g / 2oz butter
Wine vinegar
A small handful of fresh parsley, chopped
2-3 leaves of baby gem lettuce per person, washed

First make your 'weave'. Finely dice the shallot and the chilli, crush the garlic, and sauté them together in a little olive oil on a low heat. You're not looking for any colour – just soften them for 5-10 minutes. Now stir through the cayenne, cumin and Dijon, pop in the bay leaf, season with salt and pepper, and cook out for another few minutes to let the aromatics open up. Set aside.

Put a heavy-based or non-stick pan on a medium-high heat, and add a drizzle of olive oil and half the butter. Fry the livers, giving them about 2 minutes on each side: at this stage you're mainly looking to get some nice colour on them, so don't move them around too much, and cook them in two batches if it avoids overcrowding the pan. Season each side with salt and pepper as you go along.

Once they're nicely coloured, mix in your spiced weave and add the cream. Allow the mixture to heat through and bubble up, then stir through the remaining 25g of butter until it's all melted and the sauce becomes glossy. Remove from the heat, add the chopped parsley, a dash of vinegar, and season to taste.

Serve with the baby gem leaves on
the side.

Net carbs for whole recipe is 10.5g.
For each serving, simply divide this
weight by number of servings.

Ox liver with mixed alliums

Liver and onions is a classic combination, and for good reason. This recipe offers three alternative ways of preparing onions, which enhances the flavour and texture of that aspect of the dish.

Serves 2

300g / 2/3lb ox or lamb liver
40g / 1.5oz of butter
2 white onions
6 cloves of garlic
100ml / 1/2 cup chicken stock
Half a red onion
6 spring onions, trimmed and washed
2 big handfuls of fresh parsley
A lemon

First make the onion soubise. Finely slice the white onions. Melt the butter in a pot and add the onions plus the garlic, peeled but otherwise intact. Season with salt and sweat down for 5 minutes on a low-medium heat, being sure not to let them take on any colour.

Pour in the chicken stock and allow to cook down on a simmer until the onions are more or less collapsed and the liquid quite reduced. Remove from the heat and use a stick blender to blitz it up. You want it to be nice and thick here, so if it still seems a little thin reduce it down further. Set aside.

Get a heavy-bottomed or non-stick frying pan smoking hot, then sear the ox livers in a drizzle of olive oil and a small knob of butter, turning the heat down a notch to medium-high once they're in the pan. Season both sides with salt and pepper as you go along. Each side will need 2-3 minutes, depending on how thick the livers are and how pink you like it inside. Once they're cooked to your liking, remove to a warm plate.

Tip out the fat from the pan, then grill the spring onions in a little fresh olive oil, turning occasionally. They'll need 3-4 minutes, but keep turning them to ensure an even cooking. Don't be afraid of the odd dark patch.

Peel and finely slice the red onion and place in a bowl. Pick the parsley leaves from the stalks and add to the bowl. Zest around half the lemon in there, squeeze in plenty of juice, and season well with salt and pepper. Now scrunch everything up with one hand, so that the salt and lemon get into the onions and herbs and start to break them down. Drizzle in some olive oil and add the spring onions, tossing them around so that they mop up their share of the dressing.

To serve, reheat the soubise and spread over the bottom of the plate. Slice up the liver and layer it across this, then top with the onion salad.

Net carbs for whole recipe is 48.9g. For each serving, simply divide this weight by number of servings.

Liver pâté

Another traditional way to eat liver. This is rich and filling, and very simple to prepare. Feel free to add extra beef dripping or butter while blitzing, bearing in mind that they'll alter the texture once set.

200g smoked streaky bacon
450g / 1lb ox or lambs liver
1 small white onion
4 cloves of garlic
2 tbsp chopped rosemary
2 tbsp thyme leaves
50g / 2oz butter or beef dripping
3 tbsp extra virgin olive oil
3 tbsp balsamic vinegar

Cut the bacon into 1cm strips and fry them in the butter or dripping until crispy, then transfer to a bowl. On a medium-high heat, fry the liver in the same pan, seasoned with salt and pepper. Add extra fat if necessary.

Cook until nicely coloured on the outside and still a little tender on the inside. If you feel unsure about cooking offal, simply cook it through. When finished, place in a food processor.

Finely dice the onion and sweat off in the same pan on a low-medium heat, seasoned with salt and pepper (if you used butter, you may have to refresh it; if you used dripping, it will be fine, but add more if required).

Finely chop the garlic and add it to the pan along with the herbs once the onions have softened and gone translucent. Cook out for a further 2 minutes. If you have some brandy or port to hand, add a big glug now and allow to reduce to almost nothing. If not, add the balsamic vinegar to deglaze the pan, scraping at the bottom to release anything that's stuck.

Transfer the contents of the pan to the food processor along with the liver and the olive oil, and blend until completely smooth, stopping halfway to scrape down the sides (some supermarkets do a cheap truffle infused olive oil - try that out in this recipe if you see it). When it's smooth, add all but a few pieces of the bacon and pulse for a few seconds or so, just in order to incorporate the bacon and give the pate some texture.

Lastly check for seasoning, adding

more salt, pepper or balsamic vinegar to taste.

To serve, garnish with the last of the bacon pieces alongside slices of celery and carrot.

Net carbs for whole recipe is 30.3g. For each serving, simply divide this weight by number of servings.

Smoked haddock with leeks, spinach and cream
Smoked fish with poached eggs and rocket
Smoked mackerel pate
Butterflied sardines with tomatoes and olives
Steamed fish parcel
Herrings with cucumber, yogurt and dill salad
Rainbow trout with broccoli and buttered almonds
Pan-fried mackerel with beetroot, red cabbage and horseradish
Prawn cocktail with grilled gem lettuce and avocado
Hake 'acqua pazza'
Poached fish with vierge dressing

Rich in omega 3 fatty acids and essential minerals, fish is an invaluable source of nutritional goodness, and getting more of it into your diet is of great benefit. It's also a delight to cook, often allowing you to combine delicate preparation with more robust flavour combinations – there's something unrivalled about a well-rounded fish dish. Freshness is of course paramount, but fish both freezes and preserves well, so always keep an eye out for smoked, confited and salted options. To get the best price, chat to your local fishmonger about what's plentiful and in season. These recipes offer a variety of ways of cooking fish – pan-fried, grilled, poached, steamed – and don't forget the entries in the chapters on eggs and soups for some further ideas.

Smoked haddock with leeks, spinach & cream

Smoked haddock and cream were made for each other, giving a rich, moreish warmth that will leave you fully sated.

Serves 2

2 fillets of smoked haddock, pin-boned and skinned
200ml / 3/4 cup double cream / heavy whipping cream
2 big knobs of butter
1 small leek, sliced in rounds
300g / 2/3lb baby spinach (around half a bag)
A lemon
A small handful of fresh herbs, such as chives, parsley or dill

Wash the leeks and spinach separately in plenty of cold water then leave to drip dry in colanders.

Put a pot of water onto boil. When it's up, salt it, add the leeks, and simmer gently until you can pierce them with a knife – around 5 minutes. Use a slotted spoon to lift them into a colander when ready.

Put a grill on high heat and place the haddock fillets on a tray. Pour the cream over them, sit a knob of butter on top of each fillet, and sprinkle with black pepper. Place under the grill and cook for around 5 minutes, or until the fish begins to flake easily, and you can feel that the inside is heated. At this point, the cream should have begun to blister and take on some colour too.

While the fish is cooking, put a pan on a medium heat, add a small knob of butter or some olive oil, and return the leeks to the heat. Once they start to warm up, add the washed spinach, season everything with salt and pepper, and allow the leaves to start wilting down. Once the fish is cooked, remove from the grill, squeeze over some lemon juice, and pour the creamy sauce into the leeks and spinach.

To serve, stir the fresh herbs through the leeks and spinach and divide the vegetables between two plates. Place the fish on top, then drizzle the creamy sauce around it, along with a squeeze of lemon juice.

Net carbs for whole recipe is 21.7g. For each serving, simply divide this weight by number of servings.

Smoked fish with poached eggs & rocket

This is a quick lunch or light dinner that will only take you as long as poaching some eggs. The smoked fish could also be replaced by any tinned fish.

Serves 2

2 tbsp pumpkin seeds
200g / 7oz hot-smoked fish of your choice, e.g. mackerel, salmon
4 eggs
Some fresh rocket or lambs lettuce
1 tbsp crème fraiche / sour cream
A lemon

In a small frying pan, toast the pumpkin seeds in a dribble of olive oil on a low-medium heat until they colour and start to pop, then set aside.

Meantime put a pan of water onto boil for the eggs. Adding a dash of white vinegar will help poach them in a nice shape. Once the water's boiling, crack in the eggs, and set a timer for 3 minutes.

While the eggs are poaching, put the crème fraiche, a big squeeze of lemon juice and a large glug of olive oil into a mixing bowl. Whisk together briefly, then break the fish into this. Toss all this together, then season with salt and plenty of cracked black pepper.

When you're happy with the taste, add in the rocket and pumpkin seeds and toss around again in order to coat the leaves with the dressing and distribute the fish and seeds. Divide between two plates.

When the eggs are ready, remove them to a cloth or piece of kitchen paper to soak up excess poaching liquor. Season with salt and pepper, sit on top of the salad, and crack open.

Net carbs for whole recipe is 3.5g. For each serving, simply divide this weight by number of servings.

Smoked mackerel pâté

This is a super simple recipe, but you'll need a food processor to do it. It's great with raw vegetables like radishes, carrots or celery.

Serves 2, with some leftover

200g / 7oz hot smoked mackerel
150g / 2/3 cup butter, cubed
50-100g / 2-4oz crème fraiche / sour cream
A lemon

Put the cubed butter and the mackerel, broken down a little, into the food processor and blitz until smooth.
If necessary, scrape down the sides before adding 50g of crème fraiche and the juice of half the lemon. Blitz only briefly until everything is blended and smooth. Feel free to thin it out with more crème fraiche if you like. Check for seasoning and adjust to your taste with salt, pepper and lemon juice.

Net carbs for whole recipe is 4g. For each serving, simply divide this weight by number of servings.

Butterflied sardines with tomatoes & olives

This is such a simple and pleasing dish that will make you want to eat outside.

Serves 2

2-3 whole sardines, butterflied (ask your fishmonger to do this)
3 ripe tomatoes
Dried oregano
40g / 1.5oz olives (whichever colour or type you like)
1 clove of garlic
2 anchovies
1 tbsp capers
Olive oil
A lemon

First prepare the garnish, so that the flavours have a chance to develop. Slice the tomatoes across the way to whatever thickness you like, and toss them in a bowl with some salt and pepper, a good glug of olive oil, and a pinch or two of oregano. Divide the tomatoes equally between two plates, and leave to sit.

Now make your tapenade. Mash the garlic and anchovies with the flat of your knife, then chop the olives and capers to a consistency you're happy with, and combine the two in a bowl with enough olive oil to make something you can loosely scatter. Season with salt to taste – it won't need much given the nature of the ingredients – and a good squeeze of lemon juice.

To cook the fish, place a non-stick or cast-iron pan on a high heat and allow it to get smoking hot. It's difficult for a pan to be too hot for cooking fish with its skin on, so don't feel anxious about this. Once it's heated, drizzle in a little olive oil and then – with a fish slice at the ready – place a whole sardine skin-side-down in the pan. Immediately use the back of the fish slice to press the fish against the base of the pan, and hold it there for 5-10 seconds. It may seem counter-intuitive, but this ultimately helps to prevent the skin from sticking. Now repeat this with the other fish.

Leave the sardines to cook without touching them for around 2-3 minutes, or until you can see that all but the top fifth of the fish has cooked form the bottom-up. If they're not already moving around when you shake the pan, work your way around the edges of each fish using your fish slice in order to release them from the bottom of the pan.

Flip them over, give them 10 seconds each on the flesh side, then place them skin-side-up on top of your tomatoes. Season lightly, and give them a generous squeeze of lemon juice.
Drizzle over your olive dressing and serve.

Net carbs for whole recipe is 13.1g. For each serving, simply divide this weight by number of servings.

Steamed fish parcel

These are a great all-in-one option that can be prepared a little ahead of time too, ready to pop in the oven when you get home from work. You can play around with the flavours here too – try adding some ginger, lemongrass and chilli for something more fragrant.

Feeds 2

2 fillets of fish of your choice, fresh or frozen, e.g. plaice, pollock, hake
6 spring onions
A handful of fresh herbs like parsley, chives or dill
2 large knobs of butter, softened
A lemon
Tin foil

Set the oven to 180C / Fan 160 / Gas 4 / 350F.

First make the parcels – you'll need one per portion. Judge by the size of your fish how big they need to be. Cut a square of tinfoil that will wrap around each fillet, but not tightly. You need to be able to seal up all the edges by scrunching the tinfoil together in order to trap the steam inside and cook the fish.
Sit the fillets on top of the tinfoil squares, smear a large knob of butter over each, season with salt and pepper, and place a round slice of lemon on top.

Lay the spring onions over the fish, then sprinkle with your herbs. Squeeze over a little lemon juice, add a tablespoon of water, and then begin to seal up the parcel.

Place the parcels on a baking tray, and cook according to the thickness of the fish – anywhere from 4-5 minutes for a flat fish like plaice, and up to 9-10 minutes for a thicker fish. With practice you'll be able to find the right cooking time and degree for you.

Bear in mind that frozen fish will take longer. If using this, it's a good idea to prepare the parcels in the morning, leave in the fridge, and bake in the evening, when the fish will have largely defrosted.

To serve, remove from the oven, place the parcels on a plate, open up, and eat directly from the foil.

Net carbs for whole recipe is 6.2g. For each serving, simply divide this weight by number of servings.

Herrings with cucumber, yogurt & dill salad

When they're in season, herrings are inexpensive and delicious. Ask your fishmonger to butterfly them for you.

Serves 2

2-3 whole herrings, butterflied
A quarter of a large cucumber
1 banana shallot
Greek-style yogurt
A small handful of fresh dill
A lemon
White wine or cider vinegar

First make the garnish. Split the cucumber lengthwise and remove the watery seeds with a teaspoon. Halve each lengthwise again, then dice it up.

Peel and halve the shallot, then slice finely and place in a colander with the cucumber. Salt the vegetables well, toss around together, then leave for 15 minutes. Once this time's up, rinse with water and leave to drain for another 10 minutes.

Mix the cucumber and shallot with enough yogurt just to loosen them, then add the fresh dill, some lemon juice, a small splash of vinegar, and season with black pepper – it shouldn't need more salt, but check just in case.

Place a heavy-bottomed or non-stick frying pan on a high heat, and season the skin side of the herrings with salt. Once the pan is hot, drizzle in a little olive oil and place the fish skin-side-down, pressing it against the pan with a fish slice for 5-10 seconds. Allow the fish to cook almost fully in this way without moving it around, then flip it for a final few seconds. Overall it should only take around 3 minutes.

Remove the fish onto a plate, squeeze over some lemon juice, and place the salad alongside it.

Net carbs for whole recipe is 20.7g. For each serving, simply divide this weight by number of servings.

Rainbow trout with broccoli & buttered almonds

Fish with buttery almonds is a favourite of mine, and the addition of broccoli (or cauliflower) creates a great combination of textures.

Serves 2

2 fillets of rainbow trout
Half a large broccoli, broken into florets
2 heaped tbsp flaked almonds
50g / 1/4 cup butter
2 anchovies
A lemon

Start with the almonds. Melt the butter in a small frying pan then add the nuts. On a low-medium heat, allow the butter to foam. The nuts will begin to brown, and the loveliest aroma will come as the nuts become buttery and the butter turns nutty. When you're satisfied with the colour of the almonds, strain them off, reserving the butter.

Bring a pot of water to the boil for blanching the broccoli. When it's up, season with salt and add the broccoli. Give it anywhere from 2 to 5 minutes, depending how soft you like it. Strain off and leave to drip dry in a colander.

While this is happening, put a non-stick or heavy-bottomed frying pan on high heat for the fish, and have a fish slice on hand. When the pan begins to smoke, drizzle in some olive oil and place your trout fillets in skin-side-down. Immediately use the back of the fish slice to press the fish against the base of the pan, and hold it there for 5-10 seconds. Now repeat this with the other fillet.

Leave the trout to cook without touching them for around 2-3 minutes, or until you can see that all but the top fifth of the fish has cooked form the bottom-up. If they're not already moving around when you shake the pan, work your way around the edges of each fish using your fish slice in order to release them from the bottom of the pan. Add a small knob of butter, flip the fish over, and give them 10 seconds on the flesh side.

Remove to a warmed plate and add the anchovy and almonds to the pan, along with a drizzle of the butter you fried the almonds in. Once the anchovy has broken up, add the broccoli, season with salt and pepper, and toss everything around. Allow to warm and mingle on a medium heat for a couple of minutes, depending on how cool your broccoli had become, then squeeze over some lemon juice.

To serve, spoon some of the broccoli and almonds onto the centre of a plate, place the fish skin-side-up on top, then drizzle with any buttery juices from the pan and a squeeze of lemon juice.

Net carbs for whole recipe is 20.3g. For each serving, simply divide this weight by number of servings.

Pan-fried mackerel with beetroot, red cabbage & horseradish

It takes some practice to get the perfect sear on a mackerel fillet, but once you get there this inexpensive oily fish becomes unrivalled. It works especially well with heat, but if horseradish isn't for you then try it with a spoonful of harissa and a shaved carrot salad.

Serves 2

2 fillets of mackerel
1 beetroot
1/8 of a red cabbage
1 jar of horseradish cream
A small handful of fresh herbs such as parsley, dill or chives

First prepare the salad. Peel the beetroot and grate it into a bowl. Remove the outer layer of the cabbage and cut away any thick stalk. You can grate the cabbage too, but it looks nicer if you slice it up as finely as you can with a sharp knife.

Mix the beetroot and cabbage together with a good glug of olive oil, season with salt and pepper, and stir through the freshly chopped herbs. Allow the salad to mingle while you cook your fish.

Place a non-stick or cast-iron pan on a high heat, and allow it to get smoking hot. Make three parallel incisions in the skin a couple of centimetres apart, and season with salt. Once the pan is hot, drizzle in a little olive oil, then place the mackerel skin-side-down in the pan, one fillet at a time. Immediately use the back of a fish slice to press the fish against the base of the pan, and hold it there for 5-10 seconds.

Leave the fillets to cook without touching them for around 3 minutes, or until you can see that all but the top fifth of the fish has cooked form the bottom-up. If they're not already moving around when you shake the pan, work your way around the edges of each fish using your fish slice in order to release them from the bottom of the pan.

Carefully flip the fish and give them a few seconds to finish cooking on the other side, then remove to a plate and squeeze over some lemon juice.

To serve, place a portion of salad on each plate, lay a mackerel fillet by its side, and add a dollop of horseradish cream.

Net carbs for whole recipe is 27.6g. For each serving, simply divide this weight by number of servings.

Prawn cocktail with grilled gem lettuce & avocado

Frozen prawns are relatively inexpensive and quick to defrost for this impromptu light meal.

Serves 2

200g / 7oz defrosted prawns
1 head of baby gem lettuce
1 ripe avocado
A lemon
1-2 tbsp mayonnaise (see p.160)
¼ tsp smoked paprika
Tabasco

Put a griddle pan or regular frying pan on a medium-high heat.
In a bowl, mix the mayonnaise with the smoked paprika and then stir through the prawns. Season to taste with salt, lemon juice and tabasco. If you prefer it looser, add some extra mayonnaise. Set aside.

Slice the gem lettuce in quarters lengthways, and brush the cut sides with olive oil. Once the pan's hot, lay the lettuce oil-side-down in the pan. Leave it there for 2-3 minutes, or until it's taken on colour, then flip onto the other oiled side and repeat. Don't be afraid to let it darken as if it were on a BBQ. Remove to a plate, season with salt, some extra olive oil and a squeeze of lemon juice.

Halve the avocado, remove the stone, and slip the flesh from the skin using a spoon. Slice it up whichever way you like and dress with olive oil, lemon juice and salt.

Arrange the avocado over the grilled lettuce and top with the prawns.

Net carbs for whole recipe is 10.8g. For each serving, simply divide this weight by number of servings.

Hake 'acqua pazza'

Acqua pazza means 'crazy water' in Italian, and refers to the method of poaching white fish in a flavoured broth. That's not exactly how this recipe goes, but it is crazy good, and a perfect use of juicy, ripe tomatoes. Feel free to use any white fish, frozen or fresh, such as pollock, coley or cod.

Serves 2

2 portions of hake fillet, skin on
3 ripe tomatoes
2 cloves of garlic
1 tbsp capers
A small handful of fresh basil
A lemon

Pre-heat the oven to 200 degrees.

Roughly chop the tomatoes into chunks and put in a bowl. If you're using cherry tomatoes, just halve them. Skin and crush the garlic and add to the bowl along with the capers, and a couple of big glugs of olive oil.

Season the tomatoes well with salt and pepper, give it all a good mix, and set aside so that the flavours get to know each other and the tomatoes start to macerate.

Meanwhile put a non-stick or heavy-bottomed frying pan on a high heat. Season the fish on the skin side with salt, patting them dry first if they're wet. Once the pan is hot, drizzle in a little olive oil, then place the fish fillets skin-side-down in the pan, one fillet at a time. Immediately use the back of a fish slice to press the fish against the base of the pan, and hold it there for 5-10 seconds. Turn the heat down a little to medium, and give them 5 minutes before checking: you want the skin to evenly take on some colour and start crisping up.

Carefully flip the fillets over onto the flesh side and pour the juicy tomato mixture into the pan, around the fish rather than on top of it. It will bubble up then calm down. Allow it to come to a simmer, then place the pan in the oven, uncovered, for around 5 minutes. The time it takes will depend on the size of your fillets – it should still have a slight give when you squeeze the sides to check.

Once cooked, remove from the

oven, tear up the basil and stir into the sauce, and give everything a good squeeze of lemon juice. Divide between plates to serve, with an extra glug of olive oil.

Net carbs for whole recipe is 12.9g. For each serving, simply divide this weight by number of servings.

Poached fish with vierge dressing

You can use just about any fish for this, and it's a good recipe for frozen fish (defrost it first). Otherwise, something like skate wing is great, and tends to be inexpensive. Vierge is a dressing served warm, so it can be prepared in a pan and drizzled straight over your freshly poached fish.

Serves 2

2 portions of fish
1 ripe tomato
Half a small red onion
1 tbsp capers
A lemon
A small handful of fresh parsley
Red wine vinegar
2 big handfuls of baby spinach

Put a pan of water on to boil. While it's coming up, make your dressing. Quarter and de-seed the tomato, then dice it up quite small. Finely slice the red onion.

Put both of these in a small pot with a good layer of extra virgin olive oil, a tablespoon of red wine vinegar, and the capers. Season with salt and pepper and warm everything through on a low-medium heat. All you're looking for here is to take the rawness off the onions and allow the flavours to mingle: from the point at which it starts to sizzle a little, give it 2 minutes, then add the parsley and a squeeze of lemon juice and remove from the heat.

When the water's up, season well with salt and place the fish in it. How long it takes will depend entirely on what type of fish you're using and how thick the cut is. As ever with fish, cooking it all the way through won't give you the best texture, so err on the side of under and continue checking. Once it's done, remove with a slotted spoon onto a plate and pour out all but a thin layer of the water (remove any scum that may have gathered). Drizzle in some olive oil, turn up the heat, and pop in the spinach. Allow it to start wilting, then add a squeeze of lemon juice and stir around to coat it.

To serve, place some spinach on the side of the fish and drizzle over the warm dressing.

Net carbs for whole recipe is 8.1g. For each serving, simply divide this weight by number of servings.

EGGS

Boiled eggs with roast aubergine, chillies & tahini sauce
Egg mayonnaise with radishes
Fried eggs with chorizo
Poached eggs with caponata
Boiled eggs with tuna, anchovies & olives

Eggs in all their forms are not only the perfect meal from a nutritional standpoint – packed as they are with vitamins and minerals – they're cheap, hugely versatile, and provide options for meals and snacks throughout the whole day. We recommend using free-range and organic eggs where possible. See the chapters on fish, soups, leftovers and desserts for some other ideas with eggs.

Boiled eggs with roast aubergine, chillies & tahini sauce

This is a take on sabich, an Israeli sandwich, with the pita bread omitted to make a stand-alone lunch or dinner, depending on your appetite. There's something about the combination of these ingredients that harmonises so well – mellow, punchy, spicy and colourful. Take some liberty with varying your proportions here, depending on how you like the balance tipped – personally I can't get enough chilli on this one.

Feeds 2

4 free-range eggs
1 large aubergine / eggplant
4 red chillies
2 cloves of garlic
½ teaspoon ground cumin
1 tsp honey
2 lemons
1 tbsp tahini
2 tbsp full-fat yogurt (natural or Greek-style)
1 tbsp extra virgin olive oil
A small handful of fresh parsley or coriander

Heat the oven to 220C / Fan 200 / Gas 7 / 425F.

Slice the aubergine into thick rounds, lay flat on a baking tray, brush with olive oil on both sides, and season with salt. Roast until they develop a nice dark golden colour, which should take around 20-30 minutes (it will depend a little on how thickly you cut them). Remove from the oven and allow to cool.

While the aubergines are cooking, bring a pot of water to boil for the eggs. Give them 6-8 minutes, depending on whether you like them runny (6) or hard (8) or somewhere in between (7). The water should be on a rolling boil the whole time. After this time, remove the pan from the heat, place it under a cold running tap, and allow them to cool in this for around 5 minutes.

For the chillies, place a frying pan on a high heat, and put the whole chillies in once it starts to smoke. You don't need any oil. Keep an eye on them, moving them around so that they take on some charring all over. Be careful as they may start to pop. Once you're satisfied with their colour – it should take less than 5 minutes – remove them onto a chopping board, allow them to cool for a couple of minutes, then chop them up finely with the garlic. Mix this in a bowl with the cumin, honey, a good squeeze of lemon juice, and a drizzle of olive oil.

Leave everything to sit for 5 minutes, then taste for seasoning – it may need more of everything except the chilli and garlic, depending on how balanced you like the salt, spice and sweetness. It should be intense, sharp and hot, in contrast to what you'll be eating it with.

For the tahini sauce, mix together the tahini, yogurt and olive oil with 1 tablespoon of water using either a whisk or a dessert spoon until they form a smooth consistency a little like thick yogurt. Season with lemon juice and salt, and feel free to add more tahini if you like it strong, more yogurt if you prefer to tone it down, and more water if you want to drizzle rather than dollop it.

To serve, peel the eggs and chop them whichever way you like. Spread some aubergine slices on a plate, and top with the boiled eggs. Dollop some tahini sauce around this, then scatter over the grilled chillies. Sprinkle with the chopped herbs and finish with a drizzle of olive oil and a squeeze of lemon juice.

Net carbs for whole recipe is 33g. For each serving, simply divide this weight by number of servings.

Egg mayonnaise with radishes

This is a simple, satisfying dish perfect for breakfast or a lunchbox.

Serves 2

4 eggs
4 generous tablespoons of mayonnaise (see p.160)
Fresh radishes, with their leaves on if possible

Put a pan of water onto boil, big enough to fit the eggs in. Once it's boiling, lower the eggs in carefully, leave the heat on medium-high, and boil for 7 minutes.

Remove the pan to the sink and run them under the cold tap for 5-10 minutes, or until they're cool enough to handle.

Peel the eggs and mash them in a bowl with the mayonnaise. Season with salt and plenty of black pepper.

Give the radishes a wash. If they still have their leaves on, give them a soak in cold water for 5 minutes. Rinse off, and serve alongside the egg mayonnaise.

Net carbs for whole recipe is 1.8g.

For each serving, simply divide this weight by number of servings.

Fried eggs with chorizo

This is a weekend breakfast go-to for me. If you have some avocados they make a fine addition, but it's ample on its own.

Serves 2

2-3 eggs per person
75g / 2.5oz chorizo sausage
½ tsp dried chilli flakes
1 small clove of garlic
30g / 2tbsp butter
A small handful of freshly chopped parsley

Depending on how many eggs you're having per person, you may have to do this in stages.
Put a pan on medium heat and add a good layer of olive oil. Slice up the chorizo into thick rounds and start frying them, turning over halfway through, and being careful not to dry them out – they only need a minute or so on each side. They'll release some oil of their own, which is what you want to cook the eggs in.

Remove the chorizo to a warm plate when it's cooked, and crack in the eggs. Season with salt and turn the heat down low until they're cooked as you like them.

Remove the eggs to warmed plates, turn the heat back up to medium, and add the butter, crushed garlic and chilli flakes. Allow the butter to melt and give the garlic and chilli a minute, then return the chorizo to the pan along with the parsley and toss it all around. Pour this over the eggs and tuck in.

Net carbs for whole recipe is 5.5g. For each serving, simply divide this weight by number of servings.

Poached eggs with caponata

Caponata is a sweet and sour Sicilian dish based on aubergines, but you can swap them out for other vegetables if you feel like experimenting – celeriac, leeks and red peppers all work well. A plate of this is fulfilling on its own, but a perfectly poached egg, sitting atop like the burst Italian sun, finishes it off nicely. You'll get plenty of sweetness from sweating the vegetables down, but you can also add a scattering of sultanas if you like.

Serves 2

1 large aubergine / eggplant
1 stick of celery
1 red onion
3 cloves of garlic
1 red chilli
1½ heaped tbsp capers and/or
30g / 1oz pitted olives
White wine vinegar
Fresh basil, parsley or mint
2 eggs

Pre-heat the oven to 220 degrees. Chop the aubergine up into large chunks – you can expect around 16 pieces. Toss them in olive oil and salt, then roast until they're a dark golden colour and can be pierced easily with a knife – around 20-25 minutes.

While they're roasting, add a thick layer of olive oil to a pan and place it on a medium heat. Crush the garlic and slice the chilli, then slice up the celery and onion into half centimetre slivers. Fry the chilli and garlic for a few seconds, then add the celery and onion, seasoning with salt and pepper. Mix everything well and allow it to sweat down for 15-20 minutes, or until the celery is cooked. Stir it all through regularly, and try to avoid much colour.

Once it's cooked, add 2 tablespoons of white wine vinegar, increase the heat, and give the added liquid a quick blast for 1 minute. Remove from the heat and stir through the capers and/or olives and the fresh herbs. Now check the seasoning – think of this as an intense, bulky dressing for the aubergines, and adjust it accordingly.

Lastly, add the aubergines, mix through thoroughly, and set aside.

Poach your eggs for 3 minutes in

a pan of boiling water with a little vinegar added to help set the whites. Use a slotted spoon to remove them onto a cloth once they're cooked, and season with salt and pepper.

To serve, put a portion of caponata on each plate and top with a poached egg.

Net carbs for whole recipe is 28g. For each serving, simply divide this weight by number of servings.

Boiled eggs with tuna, anchovies & olives

This Mediterranean-style salad uses ingredients that are worth keeping in your cupboards and fridge at all times, and works as both a lunch on the run and a quick dinner.

Feeds 2

4 eggs
1 tin of tuna (145g / 1/3lb)
40g / 1.5oz of olives
1 small shallot, or half a red onion
4 anchovies
1 small clove of garlic
1tsp Dijon mustard
1 head of baby gem lettuce or a smattering of another salad leaf like rocket
A lemon

Put a pot of water onto boil for the eggs. Once it's up, boil the eggs to your liking: 6 minutes for soft-boiled, 8 for hard-boiled, 7 for in-between. When the time's up, run them under a cold tap until cool enough to handle.

Using a pestle and mortar, pound the garlic clove with the anchovies and the yolk of one of the boiled eggs (save the whites for the salad). Add the mustard, season with pepper, then, stirring all the time, gradually drizzle in enough extra virgin olive oil to thicken the mixture into a dressing. Check for salt – bear in mind the anchovies are salty, as will the olives be – and add a squeeze of lemon juice.

Finely slice the red onion or shallot and add to a bowl with the olives and the tuna. Remove the shells from the eggs, chop them up as you see fit, and add them too along with the extra white.

Lastly add the gem lettuce, broken into leaves, and toss together with the dressing. It may well want another squeeze of lemon.

Net carbs for whole recipe is 15.4g. For each serving, simply divide this weight by number of servings.

VEGETABLES:
ACCOMPANIMENTS,
GARNISHES &
STAND-ALONE PLATES

Roast celeriac with yogurt, lemon & hazelnuts
Courgette and radish salad with crushed peas & ricotta
Grilled broccoli with anchovy dressing
Shaved beetroot with pickled red onions, crème fraiche & mint
Grated beetroot with hazelnuts
White cabbage, avocado, lime, coriander, chillies
Braised chard with chilli and tomato
Smashed courgettes
Spiced green beans in coconut milk
Roasted cauliflower with red pepper, chorizo & capers
Raw greens super salad
Beetroot and coconut curry

There's often an emphasis on meat and fish in low carb diets, as their high levels of fat and nutrient density are unrivalled by other food sources. Unless you're committed to a strictly carnivore diet, however, seasonal vegetables, especially of the green leafy variety, will only benefit both your health and your cooking – they're rich in essential minerals and vitamins, and packed with colour and flavour. The recipes in this chapter are intended to be used however you see fit, whether as a lunch or light bite, an accompaniment to something more substantial, or part of a mezze-style spread. There are plenty of other vegetable dishes scattered through the book too – see for instance the cauliflower salad on p.23 and the pepperonata on p.60.

Roast celeriac with yogurt, lemon & hazelnuts

This is best eaten as a sort of dip, served at room temperature – it's very moreish, and usually not what people expect from a celeriac.

Serves at least 4

1 celeriac / celery root
300g / 2/3lb full-fat yogurt, natural or Greek style
2 cloves of garlic, crushed
1 lemon
A handful of hazelnuts

Pre-heat the oven to 200C / Fan 180 / Gas 6 / 400F.

Scrub and peel the celeriac, then dice it into 2cm cubes. Toss these with plenty of olive oil, season with salt, and roast for around 30 minutes, spooning everything around every 10 minutes or so. You're aiming for the celeriac to take on an even golden colour while it cooks through. When you're happy with this, remove from the oven (turn it down to 150C / Fan 130 / Gas 2 / 300F), add the garlic cloves, and use either a potato masher or a fork to crush it (don't be tempted to use a blender of any

sort). It won't become smooth, and nor do you want it to – some texture is good.

Once the oven's cooled to 150, roast the hazelnuts for around 10 minutes, or until golden.

Add the yogurt and the juice of half the lemon, and stir it all together. Check for seasoning and consistency, adding more salt and lemon juice to your liking, and potentially more yogurt depending on how thick or loose you like it.

To serve, treat it a bit like hummus: spread it on a wide plate, drizzle with extra virgin olive oil, and scatter over the lightly bashed hazelnuts.

Net carbs for whole recipe is 66.5g. For each serving, simply divide this weight by number of servings.

Grated beetroot with hazelnuts

This is a bright and punchy salad that will perk you up. It's all about the oil and vinegar, so don't be shy with these.

Serves 2 as a starter or light bite

1 large beetroot
A handful of hazelnuts, or almonds if you prefer
Red wine or sherry vinegar
A fresh herb such as parsley, mint or chervil

Start by roasting the nuts on 150C / Fan 130 / Gas 2 / 300F for around 10 minutes, or until nicely coloured. Allow them to cool before giving them a rough crush with the bottom of a pan.

Peel the beetroot and grate it into a bowl. If you have a julienne peeler or a julienne attachment for a mandolin, these are good options too.

Now dress the beetroot generously with olive oil, and take the seasoning as far as you dare with vinegar and salt – as an indication, the beetroot should be surrounded by a shallow pool of glistening gold and red.

Lastly, toss through the fresh herbs and toasted nuts.

Net carbs for whole recipe is 12.7g. For each serving, simply divide this weight by number of servings.

Courgette and radish salad with crushed peas & ricotta

It's easy to forget how delicious many vegetables are served raw – sweet, refreshing and crunchy.

Serves 2 as a starter

Half a courgette
4 radishes, washed
A small handful of frozen peas
1 tbsp ricotta cheese, or Greek-style yogurt if you prefer
1 lemon
Small handful of fresh herbs, such as basil, mint or dill

Put a small pot of water on to boil. Once it's up, add the peas and give them just a minute in order to defrost and float to the surface.

Drain them, put in a bowl, and crush them with the back of a fork (no need to get them perfectly smooth).

Add the ricotta (or yogurt), a squeeze of lemon juice, and bring everything together. Season to taste, and feel free to add more ricotta or yogurt if you prefer the consistency a little looser. Set aside.

Cut the courgette into very thin discs, on the angle if you like the shape elongated. A mandolin is ideal for this, but if you don't have one use your sharpest knife. Set these aside and thinly slice the radishes.

To serve, distribute the courgettes and radishes across the bottom of your plates, and season with salt, a little cracked black pepper, a drizzle of olive oil and a squeeze of lemon juice. Add a spoonful of the pea mixture on top of this, and tear over the herbs.

Net carbs for whole recipe is 11.1g. For each serving, simply divide this weight by number of servings.

Grilled broccoli with anchovy dressing

For me, grilled broccoli is the champion of all vegetables. Robust in flavour and a powerhouse of nutrition, I can't think of anything else that satisfies both a craving for flavour and a need for healthy food.

Serves 2 as a starter

1 broccoli
4 anchovies
1 clove of garlic
½ tsp dried chilli flakes
½ tsp dried oregano or thyme
1 lemon

Put a pot of water onto boil. Break the broccoli into florets, being sure to tear off some stalk with each piece. Set aside until the water's ready.

Mash the anchovies and the garlic with the sharp edge of a knife, and put them in a small bowl with the chilli flakes, oregano or thyme, as well as the zest and juice of half the lemon. Add enough olive oil to make a dressing of what's there. Check for seasoning, bearing in mind that the anchovies themselves are salty. It may need more lemon juice to balance things out. Set aside.

When the water's up, season with salt and add the broccoli. Give it 2 minutes, then strain immediately into a colander, and run cold water over it until it's cool. Leave to drip-dry for 10 minutes.

In the meantime put a griddle pan on high heat and allow it to get smoking. If you don't have one, a heavy-bottomed frying pan will be fine. Toss a little olive oil through your broccoli, and add it to the pan. Do this in more than one batch if need be, as crowding the pan will only end up steaming rather than charring the broccoli. Turn it a couple of times to ensure it darkens all over.

Once you're satisfied with the charring – it should take around 5 minutes altogether – remove the broccoli from the pan and immediately toss the dressing through it.

For a treat, try topping this with some grated parmesan or fried flaked almonds.

Net carbs for whole recipe is 23.7g. For each serving, simply divide this weight by number of servings.

Shaved beetroot with pickled red onions, crème fraîche & mint

This is a really simple but visually striking dish, both refreshing in the summer and restoring in the winter. It's a great starter on its own, pairs wonderfully with lamb, and contributes well to a mezze-style spread of dishes.

Serves 2 as a starter or light bite

1 pack of 4 cooked beetroots
½ a small red onion
100ml / 1/2 cup red wine vinegar
75g / 1/3 cup honey
50ml / 1/4 cup water
2 tbsp crème fraiche / sour cream
A handful of fresh mint leaves
A lemon

First pickle the onions. Boil the kettle, and in the meantime peel the onion, slice thinly, and place in a colander or sieve. Pour over the boiled water and leave to drain.

In a small pan, bring the vinegar, honey and water to boil, then allow to simmer for 2 minutes. Remove from the heat, leave to sit for 5 minutes.

Once they're cool enough to handle, put the onions in a small bowl and pour over the warm pickling liquor. Seal with cling film, then leave to pickle for 30 minutes.

While this is happening, remove the beetroots from the vac-pack and slice them into thin rounds. Place the slices in a bowl and mix through some salt, lemon juice and extra virgin olive oil. Allow to mingle for 5 minutes.

To serve, distribute the beetroot slices over the base of a plate, then scatter some drained pickled red onions over these. Add a spoonful of crème fraiche, tear over the mint leaves, and drizzle with olive oil.

Net carbs for whole recipe is 24g. For each serving, simply divide this weight by number of servings.

White cabbage, avocado, lime, coriander, chillies

Avocados can be pricey, but they're packed with electrolytes, vitamins and fatty acids, and quite often on offer at greengrocers. When they are, snap them up – their unique texture and flavour adds a wonderful layer to all sorts of salads.

Serves 2 as a lunch or light dinner

A quarter of a white cabbage
2 ripe avocados
A big handful of fresh coriander
2 red chillies, de-seeded and sliced
1-2 limes

Shred the cabbage as finely as you can with a sharp knife (it helps to split the cabbage in two parts by separating the inner and outer half of the leaves with your hands). Once you've shredded it, put it in a bowl, toss some salt through it, add the chillies, and leave it to sit for 10 minutes.

During this time, remove the stone from the avocado and scoop the flesh out from the skin. Dice into bite-size chunks and toss them in a bowl with some lime juice and salt.

Mix the avocados through the cabbage and chillies along with the freshly chopped coriander. Taste for seasoning – it may need more salt and/or lime juice.

Net carbs for whole recipe is 20.4g. For each serving, simply divide this weight by number of servings.

Braised chard with chilli and tomato

Alongside steak, this is about all I craved when I started eating low carb. If you have some parmesan in the fridge, cover it in it!

Serves 2 as a lunch or starter

4 large handfuls of Swiss or rainbow chard
2 cloves of garlic
1 red chilli
½ tsp fennel seed
150g / 1 cup of chopped tomatoes
1 bay leaf
A lemon

Put a pot of water on to boil.

To prep the chard, strip the leaves from the stalk and wash both in plenty of cold water.
Once the water's boiling, salt it, then blanch the stalks, whole, for 2 minutes. Remove these to a colander and rinse in cold water while repeating the process for the leaves.

Once you've done this, empty the pot and pour in a thick layer of olive oil. Peel and crush the garlic, slice up the chilli, and add these to the oil along with the fennel seeds. Gently warm it all up on a low heat. Finely slice the chard stalks and add these to the pot when the garlic and chilli start to fizzle, along with the bay leaf. Stir it all about, season with salt and pepper, and leave to sweat down on a low-medium heat, stirring occasionally and being careful not to let anything colour.

Once these have softened a little – around 10 minutes – add a smattering of the chopped tomatoes. You just want enough to add some colour and sweetness, and you only want the pulp, not the juice. Stir this around and let it get to know the rest of the ingredients for a couple of minutes.

Now roughly chop up the chard leaves and add these to the pot. Give it all a good stir around, season with some more salt and pepper, and pop the lid on. Turn the heat down to low and give it 5 minutes before checking. You want the chard leaves to have a slight bite, so continue cooking until you're happy with their texture.

Once ready, add a squeeze of lemon juice or a dash of red wine vinegar, and check everything for seasoning. For me this is an oily affair, so add another few glugs if you feel the same.

Remove to a plate and, if using, shave over the parmesan.

Net carbs for whole recipe is 11.9g. For each serving, simply divide this weight by number of servings.

Smashed courgettes

If you've never seen this before, it may seem an odd way of preparing a green vegetable, which we're generally told to cook until just right or else you lose all the goodness. However, it's very tasty, and complements all sorts of meat and fish dishes.

Serves 2 as an accompaniment

1 large courgette
3 cloves of garlic
A lemon
A small handful of fresh herbs, such as basil, mint, parsley or dill

Pour a thick layer of olive oil into a pan and put it on a low heat. Skin the garlic cloves, bash them up with the back of your knife, and add them to the oil. Allow the garlic to infuse the oil and soften for 5 minutes. Don't allow it to take on anything more than a light golden colour.

While this is going on, quarter the courgette lengthwise then dice it into thick chunks. Add these to the pot along with 2 peelings of lemon rind, season well with salt and pepper, stir around to coat everything in oil, then turn the heat up to low-medium and place the lid on. Leave to cook down.

After 10 minutes, take the lid off, give it all a stir through, and taste a courgette. At this stage you'll be able to judge how much longer they might take: you're looking for them to get close to mashed, but still with some integrity left. Leave the lid off and continue cooking until you're happy.

Once they're done, stir through some chopped herbs and a squeeze of lemon juice, and check for seasoning.

Net carbs for whole recipe is 8g. For each serving, simply divide this weight by number of servings.

Spiced green beans in coconut milk

Green beans are wonderful when they're stewed a little, and this rich, fragrant sauce is a great example. You can have most of these ingredients in your cupboard already, so it's a quick-fix too. These work superbly with fried eggs.

Serves 2 as a starter or light bite

2 large handfuls of green beans
Coconut oil
2 cloves of garlic
1 small red chilli
1 thumb-sized piece of ginger
1 tsp black mustard seeds
¾ tsp ground turmeric
1 tbsp curry leaves
1 tin full-fat coconut milk (400ml / 1 3/4 cups)
A small handful of fresh coriander, chopped
A lime

Put a pan of water on to boil and trim the ends off the beans. When the water's up, salt it and blanch the beans for 3 minutes, then strain and allow to drip drain.

In the same pot, heat some coconut oil on a low heat. Crush the garlic and ginger, slice up the chilli, and lightly fry them for 2 minutes. Add the mustard seeds, turmeric and curry leaves and allow them to release their flavours for another couple of minutes. Pour in the coconut milk, let it all warm up, then season, bearing in mind the liquid will reduce.

Return the green beans to the pan, and adjust the heat so that everything's simmering at a steady canter. The beans will take around 20 minutes, by which point you want to have a sauce that's neither too thick nor too soupy – add a little water along the way if needed, or turn the heat up a notch if it's reducing too slowly.

When it's ready, check a final time for seasoning, then stir through a squeeze of lime juice and the chopped coriander.

Net carbs for whole recipe is 32g. For each serving, simply divide this weight by number of servings.

Roasted cauliflower with red pepper, chorizo & capers

This is a great one-tray-wonder of a dish, full of colour and flavour.

Serves 2

Half a large cauliflower
1 red pepper
5 cloves of garlic, skin on
1 tsp dried oregano
75g / 3oz chorizo
1 heaped tbsp capers
Sherry vinegar
A lemon
A small handful of fresh parsley

Pre-heat the oven to 220C / Fan 200 / Gas 7 / 425F, and line a baking tray with parchment paper.

Break the cauliflower into small florets, being sure to tear off some stalk with each piece. Try to make them similar in size. Place in a bowl.

De-seed the pepper and slice lengthwise in around 1cm strips. Add these to the bowl with the cauliflower.
Press down on the garlic cloves with the back of a knife so that they crack open a little, but keep their skin on. Add these to the bowl too,

along with the capers, oregano, a few good glugs of olive oil, a couple of dashes of sherry vinegar, and some salt and pepper. Toss it all around and place in the oven for 15-20 minutes.

While this is roasting, peel the skin off the chorizo and slice it into ½ cm rounds.

Once the 15-20 minutes are up, remove the tray of vegetables, add the chorizo, and give everything a mix around with a big spoon. Return to the oven for 10 minutes.

When this time's up, check that the cauliflower is cooked. Once you're happy, remove from the oven, add the parsley, a few more dashes of sherry vinegar, and a squeeze of lemon juice. Toss it all together and serve, either on the tray itself or on a serving dish.

Net carbs for whole recipe is 26.1g. For each serving, simply divide this weight by number of servings.

Raw greens super salad

This is one of those fresh, full-of-goodness salads that will make you feel instantly great. Don't feel beholden to the ingredients listed here either – you can change up the veggies and herbs as you please depending on what you have in the fridge, and likewise with the seeds or nuts, whose main purpose is to provide some textural variety. The dressing just sits in the background here in order to emphasise the freshness of the vegetables, but you can ramp it up if you please.

Serves 2 as a lunch or light bite

2 handfuls of kale leaves, stripped from their stalks
Half a head of broccoli
A couple of handfuls of baby spinach, washed
Half a courgette
1 apple
A handful of fresh herbs, such as parsley, mint, basil, dill
A handful of toasted pumpkin seeds or walnuts
A lemon
2 tbsp tahini

Strip the kale leaves off their stalks into a large bowl, season with salt, and spend a minute scrunching the salt into the leaves. They'll start to soften and turn a darker green, making them easier to eat raw.

Lay the broccoli on your board and use your knife to shred off the head, so that you're left with a grainy pile. When you get to the stalk, slice it thinly and add this to the rest, along with any leaves there might be. Add this to the bowl with the kale.

Halve the courgette lengthwise then slice thinly. Add to the bowl, along with the spinach and zest of the lemon.

Core and quarter the apple, then slice each piece thinly and put in a small bowl. Squeeze over the juice of half the lemon and mix it through in order to prevent it from oxidising. Add this to the greens, along with the herbs and the seeds/nuts.

In the bowl your apple was in, put the tahini and the juice of the other lemon half. Add a pinch of salt and stir through enough olive oil to make a dressing.

Season the greens with salt (bearing in mind you already salted the kale), pour over the dressing, and toss it all together.

Net carbs for whole recipe is 59.2g.
For each serving, simply divide this
weight by number of servings.

Beetroot and coconut curry

The curry base itself here is super simple, but the spiced butter or 'tarka' really turns up the flavour. You can also blitz this up as a soup, though you'll want to thin it out a little with some water or more coconut milk.

Serves 2 as a main course

2 large beetroots
1 tbsp coconut oil
1 small onion
1 tsp cumin seeds
1 tin full-fat coconut milk (400ml / 1 3/4 cups)
70g / 1/4 cup butter
1 tsp cumin seeds
1 tsp black mustard seeds
½ tsp turmeric
4 cloves garlic, peeled and finely sliced
1 inch piece of ginger, peeled and sliced into thin straws
1 green chilli, sliced
1 tbsp curry leaves
1 small handful fresh coriander
A lime

Peel and chop the beetroot into bite-size chunks. Finely dice the onion and fry it in the coconut oil with the cumin seeds and a pinch of salt. A low-medium heat for around 5 minutes will be enough to soften it. Add the beetroot and the coconut milk, plus half the tin again of water. Bring to the boil, then turn down and simmer with a lid on until the beetroot is cooked.

At this stage, reduce the liquid a little more if too thin, then remove from the heat.

In a small pot, melt the butter, then add the cumin seeds, mustard seeds and turmeric and turn up the heat up to get it foaming. After 30 seconds, add the garlic, ginger and chilli, and let everything bubble away in the butter until it's golden and deeply aromatic. Lastly add the curry leaves, giving them just 20 seconds before removing the pot from the heat.

Pour the spiced butter into the beetroot curry, stir through and season to taste.

To serve, give it lime juice to taste and sprinkle over the freshly chopped coriander.

Net carbs for whole recipe is 45.4g. For each serving, simply divide this weight by number of servings.

SOUPS

Smoked ham hock and vegetable broth
Fish soup
Spiced lamb, tomato and aubergine soup
Asian chicken soup
Turkey, sage and onion soup
Smoked haddock, bacon and cauliflower chowder
Beetroot soup with grilled chilli and yogurt
Courgette and lemon soup with feta and pumpkin seeds
Curried celeriac soup with cumin buttered almonds

Soup is most often served as a starter, but for me it should be a big bold meal in a bowl. This is perhaps easier done when based on meat or fish, where the stock itself is so nourishing and flavourful; but there are countless ways of enhancing vegetable soups too with the right garnish options up your sleeve. Here I try to offer a sort of manual for finishing off soups that will keep things versatile and interesting, so that you're never more than half an hour away from a warming dinner that needn't cost much at all.

Smoked ham hock and vegetable broth

Nothing says soup like the deep, sweet smell of a braised smoked ham hock. This takes a while to cook, but it'll warm you to the bone on a miserable day. You can use whatever vegetables you like, of course, but this is a good start.

Serves at least 4

1 smoked ham hock
1 bay leaf
Half a teaspoon of black peppercorns, whole or cracked
1 large white onion
4 large carrots
4 big handfuls of kale, stripped from the stalks
4 sticks of celery
Wholegrain mustard
Fresh parsley, chopped

Place the ham hock in a soup pot and cover it with water. Pop in the bay leaf and black pepper and bring to the boil. Skim off any scum that rises to the surface in the process. Once boiling, turn it down to a low simmer and leave until you're able to easily pull the ham meat away from the bone – it will take up to 3 hours.

During this time, prepare the vegetables.

Dice the onion, carrots and celery whichever way you please and set aside. Give the kale a wash in cold clean water, then tear or chop up to manageable pieces.

When the ham hock is ready, remove it from the stock and allow to cool until you're able to pull the meat apart. If you're feeling impatient, you can use tongs or forks to do this while it's still hot; if you have plenty of time, it's better to just leave the hock to cool in the stock. Set aside the meat, discard the bone, then strain the stock into a clean container.

Consider how much of the stock you want to use for your soup: if there's too much, keep it aside to use for other things.

Return the pot to a low-medium heat and sweat down the onions, carrots and celery in a little olive oil. Give them 10 minutes, stirring occasionally, then add your kale and give it another 3 minutes.

Lastly, return the picked ham and as much of the stock as you think you need. Bring it up to a simmer and continue until the vegetables are nice and soft. Check soup for seasoning, bearing in mind that the hocks themselves tend to be salty because they've been brined.

To serve, place a spoonful of mustard and a small handful of chopped parsley into bowls. Ladle over the soup, then give everything a stir in order to mix through the mustard and parsley.

Net carbs for whole recipe is 54.1g. For each serving, simply divide this weight by number of servings.

Fish soup

Fish soup always strikes me as luxurious, yet it's neither laborious nor expensive to prepare. You can ask a fishmonger for fish pie mix for this, but it's also a canny way of using bits of offcuts you might have trimmed off fish in the past: store these in your freezer and make this when you have enough. A jar of cooked mussels is a good addition to this too – simply pop them in to reheat when you're resting the soup at the end.

Serves 3-4

1 onion
1 stick of celery
Half a head of fennel
2 cloves of garlic, crushed
1 tsp fennel seeds, crushed
1 tsp coriander seeds, ground
½ tsp crushed black pepper
2 bay leaves
3 tomatoes, roughly chopped
1 tbsp tomato puree
500ml / 2 cups fish stock
400g / 14oz assorted fish pie mix
A handful of any combination of freshly chopped parsley, dill, chives or chervil
A lemon

If you feel like making the stock yourself, see the recipe on p.20. Alternatively, follow the packet instructions for a cube of fish stock.

Chop up the onion, celery and fennel into bite-size pieces and fry, with the garlic, on a low-medium heat in plenty of olive oil. Allow to soften and sweeten without taking on any colour for around 15 minutes, stirring regularly.

Stir through the fennel seeds, corianders seeds, black pepper and bay leaves, and allow them to waken up for a couple of minutes before adding the tomato puree. Allow that to cook out for 2 minutes, then add the fresh tomatoes. Season with salt, place a lid on the pot, and leave to cook on a low heat for 15 minutes, or until the tomatoes have collapsed and created some liquid. (If you have some white wine handy, add this after the tomato puree has cooked out, and reduce it by half before adding the fresh tomatoes.)

Add the fish stock, turn up the heat to medium, and allow to simmer for 30 minutes with the lid off.

Once that time's up, check for

seasoning. You'll be poaching the fish in it so the salt needs to be present. If the fish isn't already in roughly bite-size chunks, cut it up, and add it to the pot. Give everything a stir through, bring it up to a simmer, then turn the heat down low and leave for 5 minutes.

Once the time's up, remove from the heat, pop the lid back on, and set aside for 10 minutes. Stir the herbs through just before serving, and give each portion a squeeze of lemon juice.

Net carbs for whole recipe is 27.4g. For each serving, simply divide this weight by number of servings.

Spiced lamb, tomato & aubergine soup

Lamb ribs aren't as meaty as their pork counterparts, but they're perfect for soup – cheap and full of flavour. As with most soups, this one in particular is best done 24 hours in advance.

Serves 4

350g / 12oz lamb ribs
1 onion
4 cloves of garlic
1 red chilli
1 aubergine
1 tin of chopped tomatoes (400g / 2 cups)
1 tsp cumin seeds
1 tsp caraway seeds
1 tsp dried mint
A handful of fresh coriander

Roast the lamb ribs in the oven at 200C / Fan 180 / Gas 6 / 400F until they're browned all over – it should take 20-30 minutes. Remove from the oven, pour the fat into a soup pot, and set the ribs aside for now.

Dice the aubergine into 1cm cubes and fry in the lamb fat on a medium-high heat, seasoned with salt and pepper. Add some olive oil if the fat doesn't appear enough. Continue frying, stirring from time to time, until it's coloured all over, then remove from the pan.

Roughly dice the onion, chop the chilli, and crush the garlic. Add some olive oil to the pan and fry the cumin and caraway seeds on a medium heat for 20 seconds. Now add the vegetables, season with salt and pepper, and sweat down for 10 minutes until soft. Return the aubergines along with the mint, stir everything together, then add the tomatoes plus the same volume again of water.

If the lamb ribs came as a rack, use a big sharp knife to split the lamb into single rib pieces, then place them in the pot with the rest. Bring everything up to the boil and check the seasoning. Turn the heat down low and leave for 2 hours with a lid slightly cocked.

After 2 hours, check to see if the lamb meat is slipping off the bones. If it's not, continue cooking a little longer.

Once the meat's done, remove the pot from the heat. If you'd like the soup thinner, add some more water. Set aside for around an hour, or until you're able to handle the lamb ribs. Strip the meat from the bone and dispose of the latter. Chop the meat up a little and return to the pot.

Serve with a drizzle of olive oil and some freshly chopped coriander, plus a dollop of yogurt if you have like.

Net carbs for whole recipe is 43.7g. For each serving, simply divide this weight by number of servings.

Asian chicken soup

Use the bones from a roast chicken to make this Chinese-style broth which also acts as a great vehicle for greens.

Serves 2

400ml / 1 3/4 cups chicken stock, plus any chicken pickings you might have
2 banana shallots
3 cloves of garlic
1 inch piece of root ginger
1 red chilli
½ tsp Chinese 5-spice
1 whole star anise
1 small carrot
¼ of a cucumber
2 small handfuls of kale or spring greens
2 spring onions
1 tsp sesame oil
A lime
1 small handful of fresh coriander

Peel and finely slice the shallots, crush the garlic, grate the ginger, and slice the chilli. Fry everything on a medium heat in a little coconut or olive oil just to soften – you don't need any colour, 5 minutes will do. Season with salt, then add the 5-spice and the star anise, and give these a minute to release their aromas.

Pour in the chicken stock (plus the chicken pickings if you have them) and bring everything up to a gentle simmer. Give it 10 minutes on a low heat.

Meantime bring a pot of water on to boil. Add salt once it's up and blanch the greens for a few minutes until cooked. Strain.

Slice the carrot and cucumber as thinly as you can (if you have a mandolin, this is perfect). Add these to the soup along with the greens. Give these 2 minutes to heat up, then drizzle in the sesame oil and check it all for seasoning.

Chop the spring onions and coriander and divide these between soup bowls. Ladle over the soup, stir through in order to distribute the garnish, and finish with a squeeze of lime juice.

Net carbs for whole recipe is 34g. For each serving, simply divide this weight by number of servings.

Turkey, sage & onion soup

Turkey legs are often very cheap, yet they're extremely flavourful and have a wealth of nice brown meat on them. This is a version of the classic French onion soup, replacing the traditional beef stock with turkey and joining it all up with sage.

Serves 4

1 turkey leg
2 very large onions
1 bulb of garlic
50g / 1/4 cup butter
1 small handful of sage leaves
1 big handful of fresh parsley

Pre-heat the oven to 200 degrees. If the turkey leg is whole, joint it where the drumstick meets the thigh. Rub a little olive oil into it, season, and roast until it's golden brown all over – it should take up to half an hour. Remove from the oven, pour the fat into a soup pot, and set the leg aside.

Peel and halve the onions then slice thinly. Peel the garlic cloves and crush them. Add the butter to the turkey fat and start sweating down the onions and garlic on a low heat, seasoned with salt and pepper. This will take a long time – up to an hour – so give it a stir occasionally. You want the onions to completely collapse and become beautifully golden, sticky and sweet.

When they're just about done, chop up the sage and stir it through the onions. Give it 3 minutes, then add the turkey to the pot. Add enough water to cover the leg, bring to the boil, then allow to simmer gently for an hour and a half before checking if the meat is starting to fall away from the bone.

Once the meat's cooked, check for seasoning and adjust as you please. Take off the heat and allow to cool until you're able to use your hands to remove all the meat from the bones, breaking it up into edible pieces. Discard the bones.
To serve, stir through some freshly chopped parsley and divide between bowls.

Net carbs for whole recipe is 40.5g. For each serving, simply divide this weight by number of servings.

Smoked haddock, bacon & cauliflower chowder

Chowder is one of those edible, transporting words. You are absolutely welcome to replace the milk in this recipe with more of the cream, and, as with the fish soup recipe (p.134), including a handful of fresh mussels (at the same time as the haddock) or a small jar of cooked mussels (at the same time as the spring onions) will add an extra layer of flavour.

Serves 2

4 rashers of smoked streaky bacon
30g / 2tbsp butter
1 onion
1 stick of celery
300ml / 1 1/4 cup double cream / heavy whipping cream
200ml / 3/4 cups full fat milk
Half a cauliflower
1 fillet of smoked haddock
3 spring onions
A small handful of fresh parsley

Dice up the bacon and fry in a drizzle of olive oil in a soup pot. Dice up the onion and celery into 1cm cubes. Once the bacon's coloured, add the butter to the pan alongside the onion and celery. Season with salt and pepper, and soften on a low heat for 10 minutes.

While that's going on, break up the cauliflower into bite-sized chunks.

When the veg is soft, add the cauliflower and pour in the cream and milk. Bring it up to a simmer and cook for 5 minutes.

Chop up the haddock, add it to the pot, and give it 5 minutes. Remove from the heat, stir through the sliced up spring onions and chopped parsley, and check for seasoning – plenty black pepper is good with this, and it may need more salt depending on how seasoned the smoked haddock and bacon are.

Leave it to rest for half an hour with the lid on before serving.

Net carbs for whole recipe is 36.5g. For each serving, simply divide this weight by number of servings.

Vegetable soups

I tend to think differently about vegetable-based soups than I do about meat or fish-based ones. I prefer to keep the soup itself relatively simple, working with a given vegetable and the addition of a spice or herb, then add bursts of flavour and texture through garnishes. From a budget point of view, having these ideas up your sleeve will allow you to be resourceful with what you've got and transform a single vegetable into something far more interesting. Here are some ideas for toppings:

Herb oil:
In a pestle and mortar, pound up some fresh herbs with olive oil and a pinch of salt. If it suits, add a clove of garlic or a squeeze of lemon.

Buttered nuts:
Fry some flaked almonds or bashed up hazelnuts in butter and a little salt. A spice or herb – cinnamon or thyme, for example – will add an extra layer. When they're lovely and golden, remove from the heat and keep in an airtight container. To serve, either reheat a tablespoon per person, or simply drop a tablespoon into each bowl of hot soup.

Pesto:
See the recipe on p.160. A spoonful of this works particularly well with all those sunny Mediterranean vegetables like courgettes, tomatoes and peppers.

Boiled egg:
Hard-boil 1 egg per person and either grate it over your soup or add it chopped up.

Pickled cucumbers:
These are a great addition to a soup, adding crunch and acidity. Dice them up, toss through some dill or parsley, and scatter them over anything you think they'll complement.

Yogurt or sour cream:
A dollop of these will add an acidic note as well as a soothing dairy hit, and will provide some bright visual contrast on many soups.

Grilled chilli:
See the recipe on p.164. This will

add a punch of heat and colour to your soup, and you can balance it out with something like yogurt or sour cream.

Toasted seeds:
A scattering of pumpkin, sunflower or sesame seeds will add a little texture and nuttiness. Dry fry them in a pan, or roast in the oven with a drizzle of olive oil and salt.

Cheese:
Crumbly cheeses like feta or goats cheese will enrich your soup – combined with some buttered nuts or toasted seeds, you're close to a meal in a bowl.

Confit garlic:
Slow-cooking whole bulbs of garlic in olive oil, with just the tops trimmed to expose the cloves inside, gives you the sweetest, most delicious nuggets of joy. While they're still warm, pop them out of their skins and store them in the oil, either whole or smooshed to a paste. Stirring this through a soup or adding a teaspoon on top and a drizzle of oil will add depth and a super garlicky hit.

Following are three examples of putting together a soup in this manner.

Beetroot soup with grilled chilli & yogurt

Serves at least 2

4 beetroots
2 small onions
2 cloves of garlic
1 inch piece of ginger
Around 500ml / 2 cups vegetable stock
Grilled chilli (see p.164)
Greek-style or natural yogurt
Fresh coriander

Peel and slice the onions and garlic. Peel the ginger and slice it into thick rounds that you can easily remove from the pot later on. Sweat these down on a low-medium heat in a little olive or coconut oil.

If you're using raw beetroots, peel and dice them up and add to the pan once the onions etc. have softened. If you're using vac-packed beets, no need to peel, just dice. Season everything with salt, then pour in enough stock to cover. Bring up to the boil, then turn down to a simmer until the raw beetroots are cooked or the cooked beets are reheated and the onions fully soft.

Remove the rounds of ginger and puree the soup in a food processor or with a stick-blender until smooth, adding more vegetable stock or water as you see fit. Adjust the seasoning to taste.

To serve, top with a dollop of yogurt or sour cream, a scattering of grilled chillies, and some fresh coriander.

Net carbs for whole recipe is 64g. For each serving, simply divide this weight by number of servings.

Courgette and lemon soup with feta & pumpkin seeds

Serves at least 2

3 courgettes
1 large onion
3 cloves of garlic
Around 500ml / 2 cups vegetable stock
A lemon
2 sprigs of fresh mint
Feta cheese
Pumpkin seeds

Peel and slice the onion and garlic and sweat them down in a thick layer of olive oil until softened. Dice up the courgettes and add them, seasoning everything with salt and pepper. Allow the courgettes to cook away on a low-medium heat until they start to soften and break down a little, then pour over enough vegetable stock to just cover.

Peel in a few strips of lemon rind and add the sprigs of mint, bring to the boil, then turn down to a simmer until the courgettes are fully cooked, which won't take long at all.

Remove the lemon rind and mint and use a stick-blender to roughly blend everything – it doesn't need to be perfectly smooth. Add a squeeze of lemon juice and check the seasoning.

To serve, crumble over some feta cheese, a scattering of toasted pumpkin seeds, and a drizzle of olive oil.

Net carbs for whole recipe is 29.6g. For each serving, simply divide this weight by number of servings.

Curried celeriac soup with cumin buttered almonds

Serves around 4

3 small onions
4 cloves of garlic
1 celeriac / celery root
1 tbsp garam masala
Up to 1 litre of vegetable stock
50g / 1/4 cup butter or coconut oil
1 tsp cumin seeds
4 tbsp flaked almonds

Peel and finely slice the onions and garlic and start sweating them down in a little coconut oil or olive oil. Season with salt and pepper. You want these to more than just soften – keep going on a low heat until they become golden and sticky and quite reduced in volume.

Meantime peel and dice the celeriac. When the onions are ready, add the garam masala and cook it out for a couple of minutes, then add the celeriac. Add enough vegetable stock or water to just cover everything, bring to the boil, then turn down to a simmer until the celeriac is cooked.

Puree the soup in a food processor or with a stick-blender until smooth, adding more vegetable stock or water as you see fit. Adjust the seasoning to taste.

For the nuts, melt the butter or coconut oil in a pan, add the flaked almonds and cumin seeds, and bring to a golden colour.

To serve, divide the soup among bowls, then spoon the almonds and cumin on top and drizzle with the butter or coconut oil.

Net carbs for whole recipe is 58.6g. For each serving, simply divide this weight by number of servings.

LEFTOVERS

Cold roast pork 'tonnato' with fried capers
Salted cabbage with pork and parsley
Chicken 'Caesar' salad
Fried eggs with spiced meat trim, baby gem & salsa
Roast beef with horseradish, roast tomatoes & watercress

There's a particular satisfaction that comes from making a meal out of another meal's remains. Thrift, resourcefulness and hunger can produce unexpected delights when they're forced to work together. All of these recipes encourage you to use leftover portions of meat as the basis of a further dinner (or lunch), whether it's a smattering of refried trim adding protein and flavour to other ingredients, or cold cuts sliced from the previous day's roast.

Cold roast pork 'tonnato' with fried capers

This is a classic Italian dish – a bit like tuna mayonnaise on another level – and an excellent way to repurpose yesterday's roast pork. It's also great for a surge of good fats, thanks to the anchovies, tuna and olive oil.

Serving depends on how much leftover pork you have

Cold roast pork (from any joint – shoulder, leg, belly or loin)
A 150g / 1/3lb tin of tuna, drained
8 anchovies
1 whole egg
1 egg yolk
1 tsp Dijon mustard
100-150ml / 1/2 cup extra virgin olive oil
2 lemons
4 tbsp capers, well drained

Slice your pork thinly and set aside.

In a blender, put the tuna, anchovies, egg, egg yolk, mustard and the juice of half a lemon. Blitz everything until it smoothens out, then start adding the olive oil in a gradual trickle. Be careful, as too much at a time can cause it to split. It will become ever smoother as you continue, and soon enough take on the consistency of a thick mayonnaise. If you feel it's become too thick, dribble in a little water while the blender is whizzing.

Remove the blender lid and adjust the seasoning with salt and lemon juice. Blitz the mixture again after each addition until you're happy with the balance of flavours. Set this aside while you fry the capers.

Heat some olive oil on medium-high in a small pot. To test whether it's hot enough, drop in a caper and see if it fizzes excitedly. If it doesn't, wait a few minutes longer. Carefully add the capers to the oil, and allow to fry for around 5 minutes, or until they have crisped up. They can turn the wrong side of crispy rather quickly, so keep an eye on them. When they're ready, drain them in a sieve (keep the oil for frying other things), and spread them on a piece of kitchen towel to absorb excess oil.

To serve, layer up slices of pork with the mayonnaise, and top with

a scattering of fried capers and an
extra squeeze of lemon juice.

Net carbs for whole recipe is 3.2g.
For each serving, simply divide this
weight by number of servings.

Salted cabbage with pork & parsley

Cabbage and pork seem to be made for one another, as in this version of *choucroute garnie*, an Alsatian recipe that combines fermented cabbage with salted meats. It's a good opportunity to use up the trimmings from any kind of roast pork, but feel free to substitute bacon or, especially, smoked sausage. It's best if you leave the cabbage to salt overnight, so work a day ahead with this – it makes sense to prepare the cabbage at the same time as you roast the pork whose leftovers you'll be using up.

Feeds 2

A quarter of a white cabbage
4 juniper berries, lightly crushed
with the back of a knife
2 bay leaves
Some leftover roast pork
1 carrot
Lots of fresh parsley

Optional:
White wine

Peel the outer layer from the cabbage and discard, along with the core. Shred it as finely as you can – if you have a mandolin that's a great help, but a sharp knife will do.

Add the juniper and bay to the cabbage along with some pepper, salt it generously, and toss everything together with your hands, scrunching it a little to start getting the salt in. Cover and leave this in the fridge for 24 hours.

The next day, the salt will have drawn a fair amount of liquid from the cabbage. Strain this off (don't discard the aromatics), and taste the cabbage. If it's too salty, rinse it under cold water briefly. Squeeze out the cabbage to get rid of any residual liquid and set aside.

Now take your leftover pork and chop it up roughly. If you're using bacon or smoked sausage, cut these into small pieces. Fry them on a medium heat in some olive oil (or lard, if you have it), stirring around occasionally until it starts to crisp up and take on colour. While that's happening, peel the carrot and slice into thin rounds.

Add the cabbage and carrot to the pan and stir in order to coat with the fat. If you have some, add a splash of white wine at this point; otherwise pour in a half glass of water. Put a lid on the pan, and leave to cook on a low heat for 20 minutes, checking now and then to make sure nothing's sticking to the bottom of the pan. Neither the cabbage nor the meat need much cooking here - the heat is rather to blend the flavours and soften the cabbage a little.

Remove from the heat, check for seasoning – a dash of nice wine vinegar will cut it a little – and stir through the chopped parsley.

Net carbs for whole recipe is 11g. For each serving, simply divide this weight by number of servings.

Chicken 'Caesar' salad

'Caesar' is in quote marks because this recipe departs a little from the classic components in order to leave some margin for variation. Make this with the pickings from yesterday's roast chicken (before you make a stock out of the bones). You can of course add other salad ingredients to this, such as tomatoes, cucumbers or peppers.

Serves 2

Roast chicken pickings
2 cloves of garlic
3 anchovies
Extra virgin olive oil
1 tsp Dijon mustard
1 tbsp Greek-style yogurt
A lemon
Parmesan, or another hard or blue cheese
1 head of baby gem lettuce

Put a non-stick pan on a medium-high heat. When it's hot enough, add some olive oil or beef dripping and flash fry the chicken pickings to give them some colour and crispiness. Cook until golden, season with salt and pepper, and set aside.

Turn the same pan down low, drizzle in some more olive oil, then add the garlic and anchovies, both crushed in a pestle and mortar (or finely chopped if not). Give them just a minute in order to get them going then pour the contents of the pan into a small mixing bowl. Whisk in the mustard, followed by the yogurt and a squeeze of lemon juice. Now continue whisking in a steady trickle of olive oil until you have a dressing consistency. Season to taste, and toss the chicken through it.

Break the baby gem into leaves, then slice these in half lengthways. Toss these through the salad so that everything's nicely coated. If you're using parmesan or another hard cheese, grate it over everything; if using a blue cheese, break it into rough cubes and toss it through.

Net carbs for whole recipe is 14.2g. For each serving, simply divide this weight by number of servings.

Roast beef with horseradish, roast tomatoes & watercress

The effort-to-satisfaction ratio here is through the roof: there's barely any preparation, but it's a fine plate of food.

Serves 2

Cold slices of yesterday's (or the day before's) roast beef
2 tomatoes
2 handfuls of watercress, washed
A jar of horseradish cream

Halve the tomatoes across the middle, brush with olive oil, season with salt and pepper, and roast in a 140 degree oven for 30-45 minutes, or until they're cooked and starting to shrivel a little around the edges.

Share the slices of roast beef between two plates and pinch some salt over them. Add the tomatoes, a dollop of horseradish cream, and a bundle of watercress. Drizzle everything with some olive oil and an extra grinding of black pepper.

Net carbs for whole recipe is 39g (depending on the horseradish cream - try to choose a low or no sugar version. For each serving, simply divide this weight by number of servings.

Fried eggs with spiced meat trim, baby gem & salsa

This is a great way to use up the scant trimmings from a roast joint of meat, though it also works well with a handful of mince.

Serves 2

2 or 3 eggs per person
A small handful of leftover roast meat per person, e.g. lamb shoulder, beef brisket, pork belly
½ tsp ground cumin
½ tsp dried oregano
¼ tsp ground cinnamon
¼ tsp smoked paprika
1 baby gem lettuce, washed and peeled into leaves
Half a red onion
1-2 red chillies, depending on your tolerance
1 clove of garlic
1 large ripe tomato
Small handful of fresh coriander, chopped
1 lime

Start by making the salsa. Quarter and de-seed the tomato, then finely dice it. Finely dice the red onion and the chillies too, mince the garlic, and mix these all together with lime juice and a drizzle of olive oil. Season to taste, then stir through some chopped coriander and allow to sit while you cook everything else.

Fry off the meat trim or mince on a medium-high heat in a little olive oil. Allow it to caramelise from the heat, and once you're happy with the colour add the spices and allow them to cook out for a couple of minutes. Remove from the heat, season to taste, and transfer to a warm bowl.

Wipe out the pan and add some fresh olive oil, return to a high heat, and flash-fry the leaves of baby gem. You may have to do this in a couple of batches, as too many at a time will end up steaming them rather than giving them a quick scorch, which is what you want. They'll take on some colour and wilt a little, but not too much. Toss them around in the high heat, season with salt, and set aside.

If the same pan is suitable for frying eggs, return it to a low-medium heat and add a good layer of olive oil. Once the oil's heated, crack in your eggs – you may have to do this in two rounds – and season with salt and pepper.

To serve, place the eggs on a plate, scatter your spiced meat over them followed by salsa, and sit the gem lettuce by their side.

Net carbs for whole recipe is 18.2g. For each serving, simply divide this weight by number of servings.

CONDIMENTS

Tapenade
Tzatziki
Pumpkin seed pesto
Mayonnaise
Aioli
Romesco
Green sauce
Anchoiade
Tahini sauce
Grilled chillies
Anchovy, garlic & rosemary dressing
Tomato and garlic dressing

This chapter collects together a number of condiments – sauces, dips, dressings and the like – which can be used in various ways, from turning a single ingredient into something more appetising and nutritional, to completing a dish with a final layer of flavour, colour and texture. The majority of these recipes can be made in a matter of minutes, and are readily available from the recommended ingredients included in the introduction. Having these tricks up your sleeve will add a versatility and creativity to your cooking that will benefit your health and your palate – we encourage you to play around with them, in terms of both matching them up with different ingredients, and altering the constituent quantities to your own taste in order to make them your own. You'll soon develop your favourite combinations and find your own tweaks, which is what cooking is all about.

Tapenade

Glistening and umami-rich, tapenade really heightens the flavour of whatever you add it to – think roast white fish or grilled vegetables.

A large handful of pitted olives (whichever colour or type you like)
1 clove of garlic
1 tbsp capers
2 anchovies
½ tsp dried oregano
A lemon
Extra virgin olive oil

Peel and crush the garlic, mash the anchovy with the blade of you knife, and place them in a bowl with the oregano. Roughly chop the capers and add these. Finely chop the olives by running your knife over them a few times – some texture is nice here so don't worry about pureeing them. Add them to the bowl too along with a squeeze of lemon juice.

Mix everything together then start pouring in olive oil until you have a consistency your happy with – keep it loose if you want to scatter it over something, less so if you just want to dollop a spoonful. Adjust the seasoning to your liking, bearing in mind the olives, capers and anchovies will already be salty.

Tzatziki

Cool and refreshing, tzatziki is the perfect foil for slow-braised meats.

Half a cucumber
Around 100-150g / 1/3lb Greek-style or natural yogurt
A small handful of fresh mint leaves, or 1 tsp dried mint
A lemon
Extra virgin olive oil

Split the cucumber lengthwise and use a teaspoon to scrape out the watery core. Grate the two halves coarsely and place in a bowl with a little salt mixed through. Leave this to sit for 10 minutes, then squeeze as much water from the grated cucumber as you can by wringing it through a clean cloth.

Place the remains in a bowl and add enough yogurt to give you the kind of consistency you'd like. Stir though the fresh or dried mint, add a squeeze of lemon juice and a small glug of olive oil, and adjust the seasoning to taste.

Pumpkin seed pesto

Pesto is traditionally made with pine nuts, but pumpkin seeds are a more affordable alternative with their own nutty flavour. This is ideal for livening up raw and roast vegetables alike.

1 handful of fresh basil leaves
1 clove of garlic
3 tablespoons of pumpkin seeds
50-100g / 1/3 cup olive oil
2 tablespoons of grated parmesan or similar hard cheese
Extra virgin olive oil

In a small pan, toast the pumpkin seeds on a low heat until they start popping and take on a little colour. Set aside to cool.

Place the basil, cooled pumpkin seeds and garlic in a food processor and blitz until everything has become homogeneous but not perfectly smooth. You may have to scrape the bowl down halfway through. Now, with the machine running, trickle in enough olive oil to give you the consistency you desire – start with 50g and add more depending on how loose you like it.

Lastly, add the grated cheese, and pulse it only until it's incorporated.

At this point, adjust the seasoning to your taste. If you have pesto leftover after using what you need, it will sit happily in the fridge, in a sealed container, for up to 3 days, though it's liable to lose its colour.

Mayonnaise

Basic mayonnaise is a ubiquitous and nutritious condiment, based on egg yolks and olive oil. It's versatile too - experiment with additional ingredients when you're making it, from fresh herbs and spices (dill or smoked paprika, for instance) to something more punchy like harissa.

2 egg yolks
2 tsp Dijon mustard
Light olive oil
A lemon

Put the egg yolks in a blender along with the mustard, a squeeze of lemon juice, and a big pinch of salt. Blitz on high speed while you trickle in the olive oil. Continue doing this until you achieve the consistency you desire, which will depend on how you want to use it. If you want to drizzle it loosely around something then add more; if you want to dollop a stiff spoonful on top of something then go easy.

Adjust the salt and lemon juice to your liking, or add some white wine vinegar if you prefer a less citric flavour.

Store in a sealed container in the fridge for up to 3 days.

Aioli

Make this mayonnaise as garlicky as you wish, and feel free to use a lighter olive oil if it's too strong with extra virgin.

1 egg
2 egg yolks
2 tsp Dijon mustard
3 garlic cloves
A lemon
Extra virgin olive oil

Put the egg and the yolks in a blender along with the mustard, peeled garlic, the juice of half the lemon, and a big pinch of salt. Blitz on high speed until you have a smooth base, then start trickling in the olive oil.

Continue doing this until you achieve the consistency you desire, which will depend on how you want to use it. If you want to drizzle it loosely around something then add more; if you want to dollop a stiff spoonful on top of something then go easy.

Now check for seasoning, adjusting the salt and lemon juice to your liking. If you like it garlicky, feel free to add a further clove or two and blitz again until smooth.

Store in a sealed container in the fridge for up to 3 days.

Romesco

This is a fast-track version of romesco – traditionally you would roast and peel the pepper, as well as use stale bread and specific types of chilli. It's delicious with brassicas, as well as with meaty fish like sea bass, cod or hake.

1 red pepper
3 cloves of garlic, peeled
1 red chilli
A handful of whole blanched almonds (around 75g / 1/2 cup)
1 tsp smoked paprika
Extra virgin olive oil
Sherry vinegar

De-seed the pepper and cut into ½ cm dices. Put these in a small pot along with the whole garlic cloves, the sliced chilli and the almonds. Pour over enough olive oil to just cover everything, add a couple of big pinches of salt, and allow to come up on a low-medium heat. You're looking for the pepper, garlic and chilli to gently cook while the almonds take on a golden colour – judge by the latter, which will take around 10-15 minutes. Keep a close eye towards the end of this time as the almonds can turn quickly.

Once you're happy with the colour, stir through the smoked paprika and remove from the heat. Tip the contents of the pan into a blender, and blitz everything together. You want it to become homogenised, but still coarsely textured rather than smooth.

Now begin adding the sherry vinegar. This is what makes romesco distinctive, and it can take a fair amount, though your own taste is the best measure. Start with 3 tablespoons and see how you like it, checking also for salt. If you'd like it looser, feel free to add more olive oil too. This is one of those sauces which can look fine when a little split, so don't worry too much about some separation of the oil.

Green sauce

One of the ultimate condiments – vibrant in colour, punchy in flavour, and versatile in accompaniment. Use this recipe as a good place to start, and vary the quantities according to your personal preferences.

2 big handfuls of fresh parsley
1 tsp dried mint
1 small shallot
2 anchovies
1 clove of garlic
1 tbsp capers
1 tsp Dijon mustard
Extra virgin olive oil
A lemon
Red wine vinegar

Finely dice the shallot and place in a bowl with a squeeze of lemon juice and pinch of salt.

Crush the garlic, roughly chop the capers, and mash the anchovies with the blade of you knife. Add these to the shallots, along with the mustard, dried mint and a tablespoon of red wine vinegar, and mix everything together with a glug of olive oil.

Scrunch up your parsley and chop as finely as you can, using your knife as if it were a mezzaluna. Add this to the rest and stir together.

Now it's time to adjust everything to your own taste. Add enough olive oil to give it the consistency you want, then check for salt and lemon juice. Judge the acidity level by what you intend to pair it with too: if you're serving it with some fatty lamb, for instance, you'll want it to cut through it, so upping the lemon juice and/or vinegar is recommended.

When you've taken it to the stage you're happy with, leave it to sit for 15 minutes or so, then taste it again – this time will allow the flavours to mingle.

Green sauce can be kept in a sealed container in the fridge for up to 3 days, during which time it will lose its vibrant colour and its acidic punch. The latter can be mended by a squeeze of lemon juice or a dash of vinegar.

Anchoïade

This is a strong favourite of mine – essentially a mayonnaise loaded with anchovies, and highly addictive.

8 anchovy fillets
2 cloves of garlic
Some milk
1 egg
1 egg yolk
2 tsp Dijon mustard
½ tsp dried thyme
A lemon
Extra virgin olive oil

Peel and bash the garlic and put it in a small pot with the anchovies. Pour in just enough milk to cover and poach on a low heat until the garlic is softened. The anchovies will disintegrate a bit, and the milk may split.

Pour the contents of the pan into a food processor or blender along with the egg, yolk, mustard, thyme and a big squeeze of lemon juice. Blitz until smooth, then start trickling in olive oil until you have a consistency you'd like – ideally you want it to hold with a bit of a wobble. If you go too far with the oil, just add a little water to thin it out again.

Check the seasoning – it will most likely need more lemon juice but not much salt.

Tahini sauce

Tahini emulsifies with water to give the most luscious and delightfully smooth sauce. It's an acquired taste for some, but once you develop a notion for it there's not much you won't want to eat it with. Start with this basic recipe and take it where you want to go: I often add a spoonful of yogurt and some olive oil to enrich it, vary the level of garlic according to what I'm eating it with, and sometimes blitz fresh parsley through it too.

100g / 4oz tahini
1 clove of garlic
A lemon

Put the tahini and garlic in a food processor with a squeeze of lemon juice and blitz until the garlic's disappeared. Add 3 tablespoons of water and continue blitzing, slowly trickling in more until you have a consistency you're happy with – keep it thick if you want to dollop it on something, let it get looser if you're going to drizzle it.

Adjust the seasoning with salt and lemon juice to taste.

Grilled chillies

I tried to recreate this after eating something similar at a Lebanese restaurant in Glasgow, where it was served as a 'side dish', but ended up getting scattered over every other mezze plate we'd ordered. Highly addictive.

4 red chillies
2 cloves of garlic
½ teaspoon ground cumin
1 tsp of honey
Extra virgin olive oil
A lemon

Place a frying pan on a high heat, and put the whole chillies in once it starts to smoke. You don't need any oil. Keep an eye on them, moving them around so that they take on some charring all over. Be careful as they may start to pop.

Once they've coloured and softened a little – it should take less than 5 minutes – remove them onto a chopping board and allow them to cool for a couple of minutes. Chop them up finely with the garlic, and mix this in a bowl with the cumin, honey, a good squeeze of lemon juice, and a small drizzle of olive oil. Leave everything to sit for 5 minutes, then taste for seasoning

– you may find it needs more of everything except the chilli and garlic, depending on how balanced you like the earthy spice and sweetness. It should be intense, sharp and hot, in contrast to what you'll be eating it with.

Anchovy, garlic & rosemary dressing

I tend to scatter this over vegetables or meat after roasting them, but it can also be used to marinade them beforehand. For best results, use a pestle and mortar.

4 anchovies
6 sprigs of fresh rosemary
1 garlic clove
Extra virgin olive oil
A lemon

Mash the anchovies with the blade of you knife and place them in the mortar along with the peeled garlic clove. Strip the rosemary leaves from the stalk and chop them as finely as you can with your knife, then add these to the rest.

Pour in a tablespoon of olive oil and pound the contents until it's all mashed together. You're mainly looking to break down the tough rosemary here. Once you've got this as far as you can – it won't be perfectly smooth – add enough olive oil to reach the consistency you like. Lastly check for seasoning – it may not need much salt, but a good squeeze of lemon juice will sharpen it up.

Tomato and garlic dressing

I love the simplicity of this, and how it turns everything to summer. Adding fresh herbs is a good option if you have some to hand – try stirring through basil or coriander at the end, for instance, or add something woodier like sage when you're cooking the garlic.

1 large, very ripe tomato
2 garlic cloves
½ tsp dried oregano
Extra virgin olive oil

Put a pot of water onto boil, enough to fully submerge the tomato, and have a second pot or bowl of cold water to hand.
Cut two shallow, x-shaped slits on the bottom of the tomato, and when the water's up pop it in for

15 seconds. Remove to the cold water and leave for 5 minutes. After that time, peel the skin away, then quarter it, remove the seeds, and dice up finely.

Pour a good layer of olive oil into a small pot and add the crushed garlic and oregano. Allow it to come up slowly on a low heat, and as soon as the garlic starts to fizzle add the tomatoes, seasoning with salt.

Allow it all to lightly cook out for 3 minutes, then remove from the heat and allow to cool. Check the seasoning, and add some more olive oil depending on how loose you'd like it.

DESSERTS

Mascarpone with berries and almond crumble
Chocolate mousse with toasted hazelnuts and orange
Lemon posset with berries
Coconut, cardamom and raspberry pudding
Apple compote with custard and nuts
Hasselback roast pears with chocolate sauce
Almond Florentines

Desserts are a tricky issue in low carb eating, and not so much because their twin pillars, sugar and flour, are the first to go when converting your diet. Ultimately, it's the desire for sweet treats at all that needs tempered, with a view to better aligning your hunger with your overall nutritional interests. We understand this is no mean feat. Cold turkey doesn't work for everyone, but neither can it be wise to have a slab of carb-free chocolate cake at the end of every meal – even if none of the ingredients are bad for you, it's far removed from the wholefoods principle, and won't do much in the long-term to keep a sweet tooth at bay. We offer these recipes to help you negotiate this matter in whatever way works best for you, and hope you get some pleasure from them. We also leave you to make the call on whether to use honey or sweetener – if it's the latter, we suggest Puresweet, as it lacks the aftertaste of other similar products.

Mascarpone with berries and almond crumble

Use whichever berries you fancy for this recipe, and of course use fresh ones if they're in season or on offer. The whole thing can also be inverted, set in the fridge, and served as a cheesecake.

Serves 4

Compote:
A handful of frozen berries (enough to garnish 4 desserts)

Crumble:
15g / 1tbsp unsalted butter
10g / 1/2tbsp honey or equivalent Puresweet / erythritol sweetener
50g / 1/2 cup ground almonds

300g / 2/3lb mascarpone
40ml / 1/4 cup double cream / heavy whipping cream
2 tbsp of honey or Puresweet / erythritol sweetener
½ tsp vanilla essence

Puresweet or honey

Put the frozen berries in a small pot with a tablespoon of water and turn the heat up to medium-high. The berries will soon release liquid, and begin to look like a compote bubbling away. It's ready as soon as it's reduced to a consistency you're happy with, somewhere between not too runny and not as thick as a jam. Once it's ready, sweeten to taste with Puresweet or honey and set aside to cool.

For the crumble, put the butter and honey in a small pot and allow to melt on a low-medium heat. Once it covers the base of the pan, add the almonds and a pinch of salt, and cook until the nuts begin to colour and a lovely smell develops. Continue stirring so that nothing burns or catches on the bottom. It should only take 5 minutes or so, but keep both eyes on it. When you're happy, remove from the heat and spread the nuts out over a plate or tray so that they cool.

While these are both cooling, whisk together the mascarpone, cream and vanilla until everything is smoothly combined and it has a pleasing thickness that is crying out to be dolloped. Add Puresweet or honey to taste, bearing in mind that the fruit is sweet too.

To serve, place a big dollop of cream on each plate and make a slight indentation in the middle with the back of the spoon. Spoon some compote into this, and top with a sprinkle of crumble.

Net carbs for whole recipe is 87.7g with honey, 18.5g if you use sweetener instead. For each serving, simply divide this weight by number of servings.

Chocolate mousse with toasted hazelnuts & orange

Chocolate mousse somehow manages to be both light and decadent at the same time, and has that nostalgic appeal of so many classic desserts. The hazelnuts can be replaced by any other nut you fancy here, and the orange, while it contrasts nicely with the bitterness of the chocolate and the coffee, can be removed if that combination is not your thing.

Serves 3 to 4

50g / 1/4 up unsalted butter
125g / 4.5oz dark chocolate
1tsp cocoa powder
1 single espresso
2 eggs
Puresweet / erythritol sweetener or honey
50ml / 1/4 cup double cream / heavy whipping cream, plus some extra for serving
4 tbsp hazelnuts
1 small orange

Toast the hazelnuts on 150C / Fan 130 / Gas 2 / 300F for around 10 minutes, or until golden. Allow to cool, then bash up a little with the bottom of a saucepan.

Semi-whip the double cream and put in the fridge. It just needs to thicken and begin to hold, and should still feel soft and ribbony.

Break up the chocolate into a bowl and add the cocoa power. Melt the butter, and when it starts to bubble pour it over the chocolate, along with the hot espresso. Let this sit for 10 seconds before whisking until everything's smooth. Add some Puresweet or honey to taste then set aside to cool a little.

Crack the eggs into a bowl with a pinch of salt and whisk until soft peaks form.

Fold the chocolate mixture through the eggs, then fold the cream through this. Divide among glasses and refrigerate until set (a few hours in the fridge, far less in the freezer).

To serve, pour a thin layer of double cream on top of the mousse and sprinkle with the toasted hazelnuts and a scraping of orange zest.

Net carbs for whole recipe is 56.1g with honey, 38.8g with sweetener. For each serving, simply divide this weight by number of servings.

Lemon posset with berries

This is a nice zingy way to end a meal. It needs time to set in the fridge too, so it's ready when you are.

Serves 2 to 3

6 egg yolks
Juice and zest of 1 lemon
45g / 1/4 cup Puresweet / erythritol sweetener
25g / 2tbsp unsalted butter
Vanilla essence or paste
100ml / 1/2 cup double cream
A handful of berries

Put a shallow pot of water on to boil – about 1 inch of water is plenty. Meantime semi-whip the cream with a pinch of salt. It just needs to thicken and begin to hold, and should still feel soft and ribbony. Put in the fridge.

Zest the lemon into a metal, glass or ceramic bowl, removing a pinch for garnishing later. Add the juice, yolks, vanilla and Puresweet and whisk together. Turn the water down to a simmer and place the bowl over the pot, then whisk continuously until the mixture thickens and becomes paler in colour. You're looking for a consistency similar to thick custard. Be careful as it will start to scramble if taken too far.

Remove from the heat and whisk in the butter until it's fully melted. Check the flavour: if you'd like more sweetness, add it now while it's still warm enough to dissolve; if you'd like it more lemony, add a squeeze of juice, bearing in mind that this will thin the mixture. Set aside.

Once it's cooled a little, fold the cream through the lemon mixture, then divide into glasses or ramekins, and chill until set.

To serve, top with some berries and the remaining lemon zest.

Net carbs for whole recipe is 6.9g. For each serving, simply divide this weight by number of servings.

Coconut, cardamom and raspberry pudding

This is a little like rice pudding, and satisfies that same desire for something warm and soothing. There's plenty of scope for adjusting the flavours here too depending on what's available or what you fancy – try poached apple and cinnamon, for instance, or add a tablespoon of cocoa. The browned butter in this recipe adds a slight butterscotch note, but if you prefer a dairy-free option, try infusing the coconut milk with the cardamom pods an hour before preparing the rest.

Serves 2

30g / 2tbsp unsalted butter
4 cardamom pods, crushed
40g / 1/2 cup desiccated coconut
40g / 1/2 cup ground almonds
200ml / 1 cup coconut milk, (if using U.S. measures, save some for topping)
1 egg yolk
Honey or Puresweet / erythritol sweetener to taste
A small handful of raspberries

Put the butter and cardamom pods in your smallest pot and melt on a low heat. Once melted, allow the butter to brown by bubbling away until it smells nutty and the solids on the bottom of the pan begin to caramelise. Remove from the heat and set aside.

In another pan, toast the coconut and almonds until they turn golden, then strain the butter in, discarding the cardamom pods and the solids (a tea strainer is perfect for this). Add a pinch of salt, stir everything together, then pour in the coconut milk.

Allow this to simmer away on a medium heat until the milk is reduced to a pudding consistency that you're happy with. Remove from the heat and immediately stir in the egg yolk (it will cook in the residual heat). Now taste and add a little Puresweet or honey to your liking.

Divide into bowls and leave for 5 minutes to cool and set a little. To serve, top with a tablespoon each of coconut milk and some raspberries.

Net carbs for whole recipe is 33.2g with honey, 15.9g with sweetener instead. For each serving, simply divide this weight by number of servings.

Apple compote with custard and nuts

If you're missing apple crumble, this will get you close.

Serves 4

3 bramley apples
200ml / 3/4 cup double cream / heavy whipping cream
2 egg yolks
Vanilla essence
Honey or Puresweet / erythritol sweetener
A handful of nuts of your choice

Toast the nuts on 150C / Fan 130 / Gas 2 / 300F for around 10 minutes or until golden and smelling delicious. Allow to cool for 10 minutes, then crush with the back of a pan.

Bring the cream to the boil with a little vanilla essence and a small pinch of salt, then pour half over the egg yolks while whisking. Return this to the pot and cook on a low heat until it coats the back of a spoon (or reaches 84 degrees, if you have a temperature probe). Stir in a little honey or Puresweet to taste.

Peel, core and dice the apples. Place them in a pot with half a cup of water, a little vanilla essence and a small drizzle of honey (or Puresweet if using). Cook down on a low-medium heat until the apples have almost but not completely collapsed – it's nice to retain a bit of texture.

Divide the apple compote among bowls, pour over some custard, and top with the nuts.

Net carbs for whole recipe is 84.9g with honey, 67.6g with sweetener instead. For each serving, simply divide this weight by number of servings.

Hasselback roast pears with chocolate sauce

There is nothing like a roast pear – apart from a roast pear with chocolate sauce. Hasselback is when you make a series of parallel slits across the flesh of something, so that the fruit or vegetable fans out slightly when cooked. If you need a rough guide, google an image and you'll get the idea. For a dairy-free option, melt the chocolate in 60ml of water and omit the cream and butter.

Serves 4

4 conference pears
2 star anise
Vanilla essence
Honey or Puresweet / erythritol sweetener
100g / 4oz dark chocolate
100ml / 1/2 cup double cream
25g / 2tbsp unsalted butter, at room temperature

Preheat the oven to 180C / Fan 160 / Gas 4 / 350F. Halve the pears lengthways and use a melon-baller (or teaspoon) to remove the core. Slice the backs of the pears almost all the way through, cutting parallel at about half a centimetre apart. Place the halves inner side down in a roasting dish. Drop in the star anise and vanilla essence (you decide how much you'd like here), a drizzle of honey or sprinkle of Puresweet, and add enough water to create a very thin layer on the bottom. No more than that, or your sauce will be too thin. Place in the oven and roast until you can pierce the fruit easily with a knife. It should take 15 to 20 minutes. Remove from the oven. If the water has evaporated, add enough to just cover the bottom of the pan and set aside.

Break up the chocolate into a bowl and bring the cream to a boil. Pour the boiling cream over the chocolate, leave for 10 seconds, then add the butter and 2 tbsp of the juices from the bottom of the roasting dish and whisk until melted and glossy.

To serve, give two pear halves per plate and pour over the chocolate sauce. A dribble of brandy or whisky would not go amiss.

Net carbs for whole recipe is 101.1g with honey, 83.8g with sweetener. For each serving, simply divide this weight by number of servings.

Almond Florentines

These are the easiest biscuits in the world, though it might take you a few tries to get the baking time right. You can make these with flaked hazelnuts too, use orange zest instead of lemon, and even dip them in melted chocolate if you fancy a chocolate biscuit.

Makes about 10 biscuits

1 egg white
130g / 1 cup flaked almonds
40g / 1/3 cup Puresweet / erythritol
sweetener
A lemon

Preheat the oven to 150C / Fan 130 / Gas 2 / 300F. Line a baking tray with parchment and brush it with some olive oil.

Mix the flaked almonds with the egg white, Puresweet, the lemon's zest, and a pinch of salt. Mix it all together, then spoon out biscuit-sized amounts onto the tray. Use a fork dipped in water to flatten them out into rounds – you want them to be as thin as possible without there being gaps.

Bake for 10 minutes before checking, and judge by their colour.

They'll colour around the edges first, and won't take much longer once that starts to happen, just a couple of minutes or so. Once baked, allow to cool for 5 minutes on the tray before removing to a rack with a palette knife.

They'll keep in an airtight container for up to a week.

Net carbs for whole recipe is 11.6g. For each serving, simply divide this weight by number of servings.